The GOD of the BIBLE

The GOD of the BIBLE

R. A. TORREY

Whitaker House

THE GOD OF THE BIBLE

ISBN: 0-88368-577-9
Printed in the United States of America
Copyright © 1999 by Whitaker House

Whitaker House
30 Hunt Valley Circle
New Kensington, PA 15068

Library of Congress Cataloging-in-Publication Data

Torrey, R. A. (Reuben Archer), 1856–1928.
        The God of the Bible / by R. A. Torrey.
                p.   cm.
        ISBN 0-88368-577-9 (trade paper)
        1. God—Biblical teaching. I. Title.
BS544T66 1999
231—dc21   99-041188

1 2 3 4 5 6 7 8 9 10 11 12 / 09 08 07 06 05 04 03 02 01 00

CONTENTS

Introduction.. 7

1. God Is Personal 11

2. God Is Spirit 31

3. God Is One in Three Persons 51

4. God Is Omnipresent................................... 75

5. God Is the Eternal I AM 93

6. God Is Omnipotent................................. 109

7. God Is Omniscient.................................. 127

8. God Is Holy 143

9. God Is Love 163

10. God Is Righteous 187

11. God Is Abundant in Lovingkindness................ 209

12. God Is Faithful 229

About the Author 249

Introduction

For many years, our Lord's deeply significant words, *"And this is eternal life, that they may know You, the only true God, and Jesus Christ whom You have sent"* (John 17:3), have occupied much of my thoughts and meditation.

How surpassingly important it is to know God! But how may we truly, accurately, and fully know Him? There is only one way in which a person may really know God, and that is by studying Him as He has been pleased to reveal Himself to us in His one Book, the Bible, and in His one Son, Jesus Christ our Lord. The greatest philosophers' speculations about God, unenlightened and unguided by the Word of God and the living Spirit of God, are futile and utterly worthless. Man cannot discover God by searching for Him merely in an intellectual way. To the natural intellect alone, God is as English philosopher Herbert Spencer long ago declared: "The Unknowable."

First Corinthians 2:14 tells us, *"The natural man does not receive the things of the Spirit of God, for they are foolishness to him; nor can he know them, because they are spiritually discerned."* But God can be fully, joyously, yes, rapturously known, even in this present life. We can know Him by studying and pondering the complete revelation He has made of Himself in the written Word and the Incarnate Word, the Bible and Jesus Christ—by studying them and pondering them under the illumination and guidance of the Holy

7

Spirit, whom God gives *"to those who obey Him"* (Acts 5:32).

> *These things we also speak, not in words which man's wisdom teaches but which the Holy Spirit teaches, comparing spiritual things with spiritual.* *(1 Cor. 2:13)*

This book is the result of my studying and pondering the Bible and the living Son of God—as revealed by the Bible—for many years. I have not been content with a careful perusal and comparison of the best translations of the Hebrew and Greek Scriptures but have gone somewhat deeply into an examination of the originals themselves. I have given much time to a consideration of questions of textual criticism,* for which I have had a great fondness for forty-seven years. My careful and minute study of the teachings of the Old and New Testaments regarding God has brought me great joy, and many who have heard the results of this study through my sermons have testified to the joy and spiritual blessing that they also have received.

Thousands of people are hungry for something of real spiritual substance rather than mere light, popular teaching enhanced by exquisite phrasing and skillful rhetoric, or made more "interesting" by an overabundance of humorous or moving anecdotes. Many are searching for the true God, the God of the Bible, rather than the false gods of today's unbiblical

---

* *Textual criticism* is a term meaning the close reading and analysis of a text. It does not imply criticizing the text in a negative way.

cults, religions, and philosophies. I hope that this book will not only be read once but will also be re-read often and deeply pondered with ever increasing joy and benefit.

—R. A. Torrey

Chapter 1

GOD IS PERSONAL

This is eternal life, that they may know You
the only true God, and Jesus Christ
whom You have sent.
—John 17:3

It is of immeasurable importance that men and women know God, that they know *"the only true God."* To know the true God is, as the above text declares, *"eternal life."* Not to know the true God is eternal death and darkness. No other knowledge is of such importance as this knowledge of God.

Today, in most of our schools, colleges, and universities, our children are being taught a little of almost every form of knowledge except the one all-important knowledge, the knowledge of God. While the Bible is the only Book in which God has fully revealed Himself, the students are not being taught the Bible or its divine origin, infallibility, and matchless value. Instead, they are being taught the crude and unsupported theory of evolution, which, as a matter of demonstrated fact, undermines their faith in the Bible.

The exclusion of the Bible from our schools and the teaching of evolution as the origin of man are undermining the morals of our children and encouraging an appalling amount of atheism, agnosticism, promiscuity, irresponsibility, and dishonesty among them. Moreover, very little of a definite and thorough nature is being taught about God even in many of our churches. Indeed, in certain foolish circles, there is a great outcry against all doctrinal preaching. Our churches are regarded by many simply as convenient places in which to address the various issues of the day and to raise funds for all manner of causes—good, bad, and indifferent. This is not the way it should be. The important thing for all of us to know and for our preachers to preach is the full truth about God as He has revealed Himself in the Bible and in His Son Jesus Christ.

The true God of the Bible is not the god of much of our so-called modern thinking, which is actually not modern at all but is a revamping of the old and discarded pantheism of centuries gone by. The God of the Bible is not the god of any of the many and ever multiplying unbiblical cults that influence our times, such as Christian Science, New Thought, Theosophy, Unitarianism, Spiritualism, Modernism, or modern philosophy.* The main purpose of this book is to

---

* *Christian Science,* founded by Mary Baker Eddy in 1866, denies the deity of Christ and teaches that sin, sickness, and death are illusions that can be done away with through mental efforts. *New Thought* teaches that through the power of the mind, one can achieve health and happiness. Phineas Parkhurst Quimby, the mentor of Mary Baker Eddy, is considered the father of the New Thought movement. *Theosophy* came from a movement that originated in 1875 and follows primarily Buddhistic and Hindu theories, especially of pantheistic evolution and reincarnation. *Unitarianism* came to

(*Footnote continued on next page.*)

make a clear distinction between the God of the Bible and the false gods of these unbiblical cults and philosophies.

In this chapter, I want to begin our study with an essential attribute of God: He is personal. As we proceed, we will see that the god of Christian Science and some of these other cults, and the god that is taught in some of our supposedly orthodox theological seminaries, is not a personal God and is therefore not the God of the Bible. Three Scripture texts will serve as the basis of our understanding that God is personal:

And this is eternal life, that they may know You, the only true God, and Jesus Christ whom You have sent. (John 17:3)

We know that the Son of God has come and has given us an understanding, that we may know Him who is true; and we are in Him who is true, in His Son Jesus Christ. This is the true God and eternal life. Little children, keep yourselves from idols. (1 John 5:20–21)

And Thomas answered and said to Him, "My Lord and my God!"
(John 20:28, emphasis added)

---

prominence in the eighteenth and nineteenth centuries. It denies the Christian doctrines of the Trinity and the deity of Jesus Christ, and ascribes divinity to God the Father only. *Modernism*, when capitalized, refers to a theological movement in the late nineteenth and early twentieth centuries that tried to reconcile traditional biblical doctrine with contemporary thinking in various fields of learning and that devalued the supernatural.

How Is God "Personal"?

First, let us discover what the word *personal* means when applied to God, or when accurately used in other connections.

What is a person? The characteristics of personality are knowledge, feeling, and will. Any being who knows and feels and wills is a person, whether he is visible or invisible, whether he has a body or does not have a body. Many people think that when you say "God is a person," you mean that God has hands, feet, eyes, ears, and so on. But having these parts of the body, or having a body in general, is not the mark of personality but of bodily existence, which is an entirely different matter. Whether or not God has a body or a visible form we will consider later on, but that has nothing to do with God being a person or not.

If the Lord does not return in our lifetimes and you and I pass through the experience of what men call "death," we will pass out of our present dwelling places, that is, our present bodies, and *"depart and be with Christ"* (Phil. 1:23). We will not get our resurrection bodies until He comes again; however, we will not cease to be persons. We will think, feel, and know great joy, for it *"is far better"* (v. 23) to leave the body and be with Him. We will, as Paul put it in another passage, *"be absent from the body and...present with the Lord"* (2 Cor. 5:8). It is clear, then, that personality is one thing, and that having a body is an entirely different thing.

One of the most common errors of our day is to confuse personality with bodily existence. I am inclined to think that when Mrs. Mary Baker Eddy, founder of Christian Science, denied the personality of God so emphatically, she was thinking of bodily existence. In fact, in her book *Science and Health*, in the paragraph immediately preceding her denial of the personality of God, she wrote, "Christian Science strongly designates the thought that God is not *corporeal* but *incorporeal*—that is, bodiless. Mortals are *corporeal* but God is *incorporeal*" (Mrs. Eddy's emphasis).

It would not be something to be wondered or surprised at if Mrs. Eddy had been thus confused in her thinking. For, in her writings, especially her earlier writings, before some person or persons who had a more accurate knowledge of the meaning of English words than she possessed corrected them, she displayed an amazing ignorance not only of the facts of science and religion but also of the meaning of words. The only exception to this was that she had caught some glimpses of things from her study of Dr. Quimby's writings, which she so shamelessly borrowed and failed to return, and of which she ultimately refused to acknowledge the ownership. It is true that she wrote, in this connection,

> As the words *Person* and *Personal* are commonly and ignorantly employed, they often lead, when applied to Deity, to confused and erroneous conceptions of divinity, and its distinction from humanity.

However, she went on to use words that seem to indicate confusion in her own mind as to the distinction between bodily existence and personality.

In any event, she certainly did obscure the great truth of the personality of God all through her writings. She constantly taught that God was a mere abstraction. She taught not only that God is love (which is true, if we properly understand the meaning of the words, which she did not), but she also taught that "Love is God," which is not true. Her teachings, carried out to their logical conclusion, lead to the radically false, utterly damnable, and hopelessly damning idea that "God is us" (all of us) and that "we are God" (not "gods" but "God").

In *Science and Health*, Mrs. Eddy said, in this very connection, speaking of the personality of God, "If the term *personality*, as applied to God, means infinite personality, then God is personal Being—in this sense but not in the lower sense." You will notice that she said, "God is personal Being," that is, of course, only an abstract Being in general. She did not say, "God is *a* personal Being," that is, a definite Person, separate and distinct from other persons, all of whom He has created. In the next sentence, she said, "An Infinite mind and a finite form do not, cannot coalesce."

This is another illustration of her extreme ignorance of the meaning of words. No one, even though he may believe very strongly that God has a form, thinks that He and His form "coalesce"; he thinks that they *coexist*. It is unfortunate that Mrs. Eddy did not have a good dictionary and study it more diligently. The correct definition of *coalesce* is "to grow or come together into one; to fuse, blend." Now, no one who believes that God has an outward form in which He manifests Himself thinks that He—an intelligent, thinking, willing, determining personality—"grows together into one" with the form He inhabits, or "fuses" with it or "blends" with it.

But Mrs. Eddy has not been alone in denying the personality of God. Professors of theology in our universities and seminaries do it also. For example, Professor Walter Rauschenbusch of the Baptist Theological Seminary in Rochester, New York, the chief apostle of what is now so much promoted as the Social Gospel, said in his book, *A Theology for the Social Gospel*, "The old conception that God...is distinct from our human life" must give way to "the religious belief that he is immanent in humanity."

Gerald Birney Smith, professor of Christian Theology at Chicago University, wrote in *Man and the New Democracy*, "The worship of God in a democracy will consist in reverence for those human values which democracy makes supreme." The natural, indeed, the inevitable inference is, if Professor G. Birney Smith had any accurate knowledge of the meaning of words, that God is "those human values which democracy makes supreme." In *A Guide to the Study of the Christian Religion,* he spoke of God as "the spiritual forces of the world in which we live." In light of this definition, he might better have called his book a guide to the study of Buddhism or Eastern philosophy. In the same book, he spoke of God as "the unseen forces of the universe."

R. G. Campbell, who was at one time the most prominent proponent of New Theology in England, but afterwards—in a measure, at least—recanted, said, "God is my deeper self and yours too; he is the self of the universe." G. Stanley Hall, president of Clark University, in the first volume of *Jesus the Christ, in the Light of Psychology,* set forth the opinion that "God is the truth, virtue, beauty of man." He went on to say that the only real atheist is he "who denies these attributes to man." Hall also said that prayer is "communion with the deeper racial self within us." Professor Royce of Harvard University, in *The American Journal of Theology,* spoke of God as the immanent "spirit of the community." It would be easy to multiply quotations from professors of theology in theological seminaries and universities that present similar pantheistic definitions of an impersonal God; however, let us turn from all this skillfully phrased foolishness to the exalted revelation of God as He is really set forth in God's own Word, the Bible.

THE PERSONALITY OF GOD AS REVEALED IN THE BIBLE

From the first chapter of Genesis to the last chapter of Revelation, we see God as a Person, an infinite and perfect Person. He is not a mere "force," or "abstract intelligence," or "the Absolute." He is an infinitely wise, infinitely holy, and infinitely loving *Person—"our Father in heaven"* (Matt. 6:9), as our Lord Jesus spoke of Him and to Him.

I will not take any space here to demonstrate that knowledge, feeling, and will—the characteristics of personality—are all ascribed to God in the Bible, over and over again. All of us who are familiar with the Bible know that the knowledge and love and supreme will of God appear on nearly every page. Moreover, we will take up all these things in detail in later chapters when we consider the omniscience of God, the holiness of God, the love of God, and the sovereignty of God. Let us now look at other important aspects of the personality of God as revealed in the Bible.

God Is a Living God

First, the Bible reveals God as a living God. Read Jeremiah 10:10–16:

But the LORD is the true God; He is the living God and the everlasting King. At His wrath the earth will tremble, and the nations will not be able to endure His indignation. Thus you shall say to them: "The gods that have not made the heavens and the earth shall perish from the earth and from under these heavens." He has made the earth by His power, He has established the world by His wisdom, and has stretched out the heavens at His discretion. When He utters His voice, there is a multitude of waters in the heavens: "And He causes the vapors to ascend from the ends of the earth. He makes lightning for the rain, He brings the wind out of His treasuries." Everyone is dull-hearted, without knowledge; every metalsmith is put to shame by an image; for his molded image is falsehood, and there is no breath in them. They are futile, a work of errors; in the time of their punishment they shall perish. The Portion of Jacob is not like them, for He is the Maker of all things, and Israel is the tribe of His inheritance; the LORD of hosts is His name.   *(Jer. 10:10–16)*

In this sublimely eloquent passage, so strikingly in contrast to the vapid word-spinning of the supposedly scholarly and brilliant seminary and university professors whom I have been quoting, God is distinguished from idols, the gods men make for themselves. (See verses 8–9.) These idols are things, not persons, things that *"cannot speak,...cannot go by themselves,...cannot do evil, nor can they do any good"* (v. 5). In contrast to them, Jehovah is wiser than *"all the wise men"* (v. 7). He is *"the living God*

19

and the everlasting King" (v. 10), a Being who has *"wrath"* and *"indignation"* (v. 10), and who is separate and apart from all the persons and things that He Himself has created. *"At His wrath the earth will tremble, and the nations will not be able to endure His indignation"* (v. 10).

The idols men form today and call "God" are not made with their hands, as in Jeremiah's day, from the wood of the palm tree (v. 5, 8), and decorated with silver and gold (v. 4). They are made with their bewildered and confused minds out of the tenuous thought processes of their own self-intoxicated musings (as we have seen in the absurd quotations given above). However, they are idols just the same, and they are not *"the only true God,"* (John 17:3), the God of the Bible.

In this quotation from the prophet Jeremiah, who lived and wrote six hundred years before Christ, we are in the realm of the sublime. In the quotations from these great and brilliant modern scholars, who lived nineteen hundred years after Christ, we are in the realm of the ridiculous. How did Jeremiah, who lived twenty-five hundred years ago, come to utter such marvelous wisdom in striking contrast to the inane nonsense of these so-called bright, learned, and scholarly thinkers of today? There can be only one rational answer to this question: the infinitely wise God spoke through him, while these modern theologians discount the Word of God and chase the butterflies of modern scholarship, pantheistic philosophy, and self-confident metaphysics. *"Professing themselves to be wise, they became fools"* (Rom. 1:22 ASV).

We do well when we imitate the early converts in Thessalonica and "[turn] *to God from* [all these disgusting] *idols to serve the living and true God, and to wait for His Son from heaven"* (1 Thess. 1:9–10).

God Has an Active Interest in the Affairs of Men

Second, God is revealed in the Bible as having a present interest in and an active hand in the affairs of men:

> *And Joshua said, "By this you shall know that the living God is among you, and that He will without fail drive out from before you the Canaanites and the Hittites and the Hivites and the Perizzites and the Girgashites and the Amorites and the Jebusites."* (Josh. 3:10)

> *And when* [King Darius] *came to the den, he cried out with a lamenting voice to Daniel. The king spoke, saying to Daniel, "Daniel, servant of the living God, has your God, whom you serve continually, been able to deliver you from the lions?" Then Daniel said to the king, "O king, live forever! My God sent His angel and shut the lions' mouths, so that they have not hurt me, because I was found innocent before Him; and also, O king, I have done no wrong before you."*...[The king wrote,] *I make a decree that in every dominion of my kingdom men must tremble and fear before the God of Daniel. For He is the living God, and steadfast forever; His kingdom is the one which shall not be destroyed, and His dominion shall endure to the end. He delivers and rescues, and He works signs and wonders in heaven and on*

earth, who has delivered Daniel from the power of the lions.   (Dan. 6:20–22, 26–27)

For we know Him who said, "Vengeance is Mine, I will repay," says the Lord. And again, "The LORD will judge His people." It is a fearful thing to fall into the hands of the living God.   (Heb. 10:30–31)

We know that all things work together for good to those who love God, to those who are the called according to His purpose. For whom He foreknew, He also predestined to be conformed to the image of His Son, that He might be the firstborn among many brethren. Moreover whom He predestined, these He also called; whom He called, these He also justified; and whom He justified, these He also glorified. What then shall we say to these things? If God is for us, who can be against us?

(Rom. 8:28–31)

My God shall supply all your need according to His riches in glory by Christ Jesus.

(Phil. 4:19)

We see, then, that the God of the Bible is not only to be distinguished from the god of pantheism, who has no existence whatsoever separate from his creation, but also from the god of deism, who has created a world and put into it all the necessary powers of self-action and development, and, having set it going, has left it to go by itself. The God of the Bible is a God who has a personal, active, and present interest in the affairs of the universe today.

God Is Personal

One of the most distinctive and conspicuous features of so-called New Theology and of higher criticism[*] is that they scoff at the miraculous, the supernatural, and the idea of God taking—at the present time or in biblical times—any active and immediate hand in the affairs of man. Many of us know by joyful and glorious experience that the biblical conception of the miraculous and of God is the true conception, and that the conception of modern scholarship runs up against the stone wall of the established facts of history and the facts of our own personal experiences.

God Is the Creator of All Things

Third, God is revealed in the Bible as the Creator of all existing things, animate and inanimate, earthly and celestial. The very first words we read in the Bible, opening the sublime epic of Creation found in the first chapter of Genesis, are, *"In the beginning God created the heavens and the earth"* (Gen. 1:1). In the New Testament counterpart to this passage, which is John 1:1–3, we read:

---

[*] *Higher criticism* is the study of biblical texts to determine their authorship and literary history, and the purpose and meaning of the writers. It deals with questions regarding the character, composition, editing, dates of writing, historical and cultural background, and collection of biblical writings. It also incorporates the techniques or findings of archaeology, literary criticism, comparative religion, and other related fields. However, higher critics often exhibit a bias against the supernatural and the miraculous. In addition, they tend to view the Scriptures as merely the words of men and not as the inspired and living Word of God.

*In the beginning was the Word, and the Word
was with God, and the Word was God. He was
in the beginning with God. All things were
made through Him, and without Him nothing
was made that was made.*

In Colossians 1:16, we read:

For by [Jesus Christ] *all things were created
that are in heaven and that are on earth, visible and invisible, whether thrones or dominions or principalities or powers. All things
were created through Him and for Him.*

All this evidence of the God of creation is in
marked contrast to the god who is left to us by the
crass, scientifically and historically disproved evolu-
tionism that so strangely dominates our universities,
theological seminaries, and public and private
schools. When you ask the educators of these institutions for some substantial proof of their theory, they
reply, "All scholars are agreed upon it." But when
you ask them about the views of particular scholars,
they reply, "Oh, he doesn't believe in evolution;
therefore, he is not a scholar." It reminds me of a
talk I had some years ago with a student at Edin-
burgh University. He had remarked to me that all
the great Semitic scholars belonged to the destructive school of biblical criticism. I asked him, "What
about Professor Margoliouth (at that time perhaps
the greatest Semitic scholar in England)?" "Is he a
scholar?" this young man asked me. I replied, "He
was considered to be until he left the radical side and
came over to the conservative side." The student
smiled and admitted that it was so.

God Is Personal

God Sustains, Governs, and Cares for the World

Fourth, the Bible reveals God as sustaining, governing, and caring for the world He created, and as shaping the whole present history of the world. We read in Psalm 104:27–30:

These all [the creatures God has created] *wait for You, that You may give them their food in due season. What You give them they gather in; You open Your hand, they are filled with good. You hide Your face, they are troubled; You take away their breath, they die and return to their dust. You send forth Your Spirit, they are created; and You renew the face of the earth.*

And in Isaiah 45:5–7, we read:

I am the LORD, and there is no other; there is no God besides Me. I will gird you, though you have not known Me, that they may know from the rising of the sun to its setting that there is none besides Me. I am the LORD, and there is no other; I form the light and create darkness, I make peace and create calamity; I, the LORD, do all these things.

Where in all the literature of the modernists or any other literature except for the Bible can we find anything that approaches the sublimity of both of these passages?

Let us look at one other passage of Scripture relating to this topic. We read in Psalm 76:6–7:

At Your rebuke, O God of Jacob, both the chariot and horse were cast into a dead sleep. You,

Yourself, are to be feared; and who may stand
in Your presence when once You are angry?
(Ps. 76:6–7)

God's Care and Government Extend to All

Fifth, God is revealed in the Bible as One whose care and government extend to all His creatures, even the smallest and the most insignificant. Read the words of Jesus in these two passages:

Look at the birds of the air, for they neither
sow nor reap nor gather into barns; yet your
heavenly Father feeds them. Are you not of
more value than they?...Why do you worry
about clothing? Consider the lilies of the field,
how they grow: they neither toil nor spin; and
yet I say to you that even Solomon in all his
glory was not arrayed like one of these. Now if
God so clothes the grass of the field, which to-
day is, and tomorrow is thrown into the oven,
will He not much more clothe you, O you of lit-
tle faith?   *(Matt. 6:26, 28–30)*

Are not two sparrows sold for a copper coin?
And not one of them falls to the ground apart
from your Father's will. But the very hairs of
your head are all numbered.   *(Matt. 10:29–30)*

God's Ministry and Government Extend to the Individual

Sixth, God is revealed in the Bible as One whose care, ministry, and government extend to the individual. As far back as the book of Genesis, the book that contains the seeds from which the whole vast tree of biblical truth has grown, we read: *"But the LORD was with Joseph and showed him mercy, and He gave him favor in the sight of the keeper of the prison"* (Gen. 39:21). And in Daniel 1:9, we read: *"Now God had brought Daniel into the favor and goodwill of the chief of the eunuchs."*

In 1 Kings 19:5–7, we read of God's own tender and personal ministries to His discouraged prophet:

> *Then as [Elijah] lay and slept under a broom tree, suddenly an angel touched him, and said to him, "Arise and eat." Then he looked, and there by his head was a cake baked on coals, and a jar of water. So he ate and drank, and lay down again. And the angel of the LORD came back the second time, and touched him, and said, "Arise and eat, because the journey is too great for you."*

God Is Sovereign Over Evil and Evildoers

Seventh, God is revealed in the Bible as One whose control and government extend to the wicked plots, devices, and doings of evil men and even of Satan himself, and as One who makes the seeming evil work out to His own glory and His people's good. Read these words from Psalm 76:10, written more than twenty-five hundred years ago: *"Surely the wrath of man shall praise You; with the remainder of wrath You shall gird Yourself."* And read these words written in the first book of the Bible, which our modern so-called scholars love so much to despise, but to whose exalted heights they have not yet climbed even the foothills: *"As for you, you meant evil against me; but God meant it for good, in order to bring it about as it is this day, to save many people alive"* (Gen. 50:20). Read also these words from the second book in the Bible: *"But indeed for this purpose I have raised you* [the wicked Pharaoh] *up, that I may show My power in you, and that My name may be declared in all the earth"* (Exod. 9:16). Turn now to the New Testament and read Peter's marvelously significant words on the Day of Pentecost:

> *Men of Israel, hear these words: Jesus of Nazareth, a Man attested by God to you by miracles, wonders, and signs which God did through Him in your midst, as you yourselves also know; Him, **being delivered by the determined purpose and foreknowledge of God**, you have taken by lawless hands, have crucified, and put to death.*
>
> *(Acts 2:22–23, emphasis added)*

Now let us turn to what many scholars regard as the oldest book of the Bible, the book of Job:

> *And the Lord said to Satan, "Behold, all that* [Job] *has is in your power; only do not lay a hand on his person." So Satan went out from the presence of the LORD.* *(Job 1:12)*

> *And the LORD said to Satan, "Behold, he is in your hand, but spare his life."* *(Job 2:6)*

In the book of Job, the Bible depicts even Satan himself, with all his malevolence, as carrying out the merciful purposes of God.

In Luke 22:3, we see the same thing: *"Then Satan entered Judas, surnamed Iscariot, who was numbered among the twelve."* The result of this act was that God's eternal purpose of redeeming love was accomplished by the atoning death of Jesus

Christ, which was brought to pass by the great enemy of God and man, the Devil.

The God of the Bible, as far as the question of His personality and His being a living God is concerned, is a God who lives and loves and acts and works today. Oh, I am glad that I have such a real, concrete, personal, living God—One in whom I can trust and have no fears, whatever may arise—and not the impersonal, abstract, vague, vapory, elusive, unreal god of the rhetorical nonsense of Walter Rauschenbusch, Professor G. Birney Smith, President G. Stanley Hall, Professor Royce, Mrs. Mary Baker Eddy, and a host of other drowsy dreamers. With such a God, I can face whatever calamity seems to threaten to overtake me and say, "I know that *all things work together for good to those who love God, to those who are the called according to His purpose*' (Rom. 8:28), and *'if God is for us, who can be against us?'* (v. 31)."

If any of you reading this desire the god of false religions or so-called modern scholarship, you can have it. I would not give two cents for it. But give me the God of the Bible, the Real God, *"the living and true God"* (1 Thess. 1:9), *"the only true God"* (John 17:3), whom to know is not only *"eternal life"* (v. 3) but boundless peace and overflowing joy every day.

Chapter 2

God Is Spirit

Now to the King eternal, immortal, invisible, to God
who alone is wise, be honor and glory
forever and ever. Amen.
—1 Timothy 1:17

In the first chapter, we saw that personality and bodily existence are not the same thing—that saying God is a person does not necessarily mean that God has a body. We also saw that any being who knows, feels, and wills is a person, whether he is visible or invisible, whether he has a body or does not have a body. Now we will take up the question of whether or not God has a body, *a visible form*. We will look at three main texts in this chapter that will give us the answer to this important question:

> *God is Spirit.* (John 4:24)

> *Have this mind in you, which was also in Christ Jesus: who, exist[ed] in the form of God.* (Phil. 2:5–6 ASV)

> *Now to the King eternal, immortal, invisible, to God who alone is wise, be honor and glory forever and ever. Amen.* (1 Tim. 1:17)

The God of the Bible

WHAT DOES IT MEAN THAT GOD IS SPIRIT?

The first thing that our texts in this chapter teach us about God—the God of the Bible, *"the only true God"* (John 17:3), the God whom to know is life eternal (John 17:3; 1 John 5:20) and whom not to know is eternal death and darkness—is that God is Spirit. This is clearly stated in our first text, which tells us in words that our Lord Jesus Himself spoke to the woman of Samaria, *"God is Spirit"* (John 4:24).

The King James Version, the American Standard Edition of the Revised Version, and the Revised Version translate this verse as *"God is a Spirit"* (emphasis added), adding the indefinite article *a*. There is no indefinite article in the Greek text. Now, that does not necessarily imply that this translation is incorrect, because there is no indefinite article at all in the Greek language, and whenever it is needed in an English translation, it must be supplied. But I think that the translation *"God is Spirit"* is to be preferred in this instance to *"God is a Spirit,"* because, further on in the same verse, we are told that *"those who worship Him must worship in spirit and truth."* Here we have precisely the same word, only in the dative case, with no indefinite article, and no indefinite article has been supplied. Furthermore, the construction of *"God is Spirit"* is exactly the same as that in 1 John 1:5, where we read *"God is light"* (not, "God is a light"), and in 1 John 4:8, 16, where we read *"God is love"* (not, "God is a love"). But perhaps it does not matter so very much whether we read *"God is Spirit"* or *"God is a Spirit."* The thought is essentially the same.

The order of the words in the Greek text puts a very strong emphasis on the word *"Spirit."* Literally translated in the word order of the Greek text, our text would read, "Spirit is God." But according to Greek usage, that would not imply what the words put in that order might imply in our English idiom. In accordance with a common Greek usage, *Spirit* is put first in the sentence for the purpose of heavily emphasizing it. The one thought that our Lord Jesus wished to impress upon the mind of the woman of Samaria was that God is *Spirit* and that He therefore is not confined to places—whether it be Mt. Gerizim, as the Samaritans held, or Jerusalem, as most of the Jews of that time held. (See John 4:20–24.)

But just what does the striking, yes, startling, sentence *"God is Spirit"* mean? What is *"Spirit"*? We must go to the Bible itself for an answer to this question, and fortunately we can again go to the words of the Lord Jesus Himself. In another place in the Scriptures, He Himself has defined carefully and exactly what He means by *"Spirit."* You will find this definition in Luke 24:39: *"Behold My hands and My feet, that it is I Myself. Handle Me and see, for a spirit does not have flesh and bones as you see I have."* (In the Greek text, there is no article before *"spirit"* here either.) It is evident from these words of our Lord Jesus that, by *"spirit,"* He means a reality that cannot be seen or handled or physically felt; therefore, *"spirit"* is incorporeal (or bodiless), invisible reality.

The same definition of *spirit* is implied in John 3:8: *"The wind blows where it wishes, and you hear the sound of it, but cannot tell where it comes from and where it goes. So is everyone who is born of the Spirit."* Now, the word translated *"wind"* in the first part of this passage is exactly the same Greek

33

word that is translated *"Spirit"* in the last part of the verse and in John 4:24. The thought is that *"Spirit"* or *"wind"* is something that you can hear but that you cannot see, and the mystery of whose actions you cannot fully solve. Therefore, to say *"God is Spirit"* is to say that God, though He is real, is essentially invisible and incorporeal.

This concept of God as invisible and incorporeal in His essence is found in the Old Testament as well as in the New Testament. We find it as far back as Deuteronomy. This is a book that the higher critics love very much to make light of. However, they have never studied it sufficiently to understand the profundity and sublimity of its divinely inspired teachings. Let us read Deuteronomy 4:15–18:

> *Take careful heed to yourselves, for you saw no form when the LORD spoke to you at Horeb out of the midst of the fire, lest you act corruptly and make for yourselves a carved image in the form of any figure: the likeness of male or female, the likeness of any animal that is on the earth or the likeness of any winged bird that flies in the air, the likeness of anything that creeps on the ground or the likeness of any fish that is in the water beneath the earth.*

The fundamental reason for the strict injunction in the Ten Commandments not to make *"a carved image; any likeness of anything that is in heaven above, or that is in the earth beneath, or that is in the water under the earth"* (Deut. 5:8) and not to *"bow down to them nor serve them"* (v. 9), is that God is essentially Spirit, invisible and incorporeal.

God Is Spirit

IN WHAT WAY IS MAN CREATED IN GOD'S IMAGE?

Since God is essentially invisible and incorporeal, the question necessarily arises, What, then,
does the Bible mean when it says in Genesis 1:26–27
that man is created in God's image?

> *Then God said, "Let Us make man in Our im-
> age, according to Our likeness; let them have
> dominion over the fish of the sea, over the
> birds of the air, and over the cattle, over all the
> earth and over every creeping thing that creeps
> on the earth." So God created man in His own
> image; in the image of God He created him;
> male and female He created them.*

If God is invisible and incorporeal, to what does
the *"image"* and *"likeness"* of God, in which we are
said to have been created, refer? Here again, we can
go to the Bible for an answer, and the Bible gives a
very definite, very clear and unmistakable answer to
this question. You will find the answer in Colossians
3:9–10: *"You have put off the old man with his deeds,
and have put on the new man who is renewed in
knowledge according to the image of Him who created him."* You will find it also in Ephesians 4:23–
24: *"Be renewed in the spirit of your mind, and...put
on the new man which was created according to God,
in true righteousness and holiness."* In addition, you
will find a remarkable commentary on it in Colossians 1:15: *"[Jesus] is the image of the invisible God,
the firstborn over all creation."* It is clear from all
these passages that the words *"image"* and *"likeness"* do not refer primarily to visible, physical (or

bodily) likeness, but to intellectual and moral likeness, likeness *"in knowledge"* (Col. 3:10) and *"in true righteousness and holiness"* (Eph. 4:24).

Here we have another illustration of what we constantly find when doing a close study of the Bible—the divine unity of the Bible. How perfectly what John recorded Jesus as saying corresponds with what is said in Deuteronomy, and how perfectly what is said in Genesis harmonizes with what is said in Colossians and Ephesians. There is a unity in the Bible that may be found from its earliest to its latest books. From where does this profound and detailed unity of teaching in the various books of the Bible come? The answer is both simple and clear: God Himself is the real Author of all the books; He was always guiding what every biblical writer wrote, whether it was Moses, John, or Paul.

DOES GOD HAVE A BODY OR FORM?

We see, then, that God is essentially—that is, in His real being and personality—invisible and incorporeal. Our text from 1 Timothy 1:17 declares His invisible nature. Let us read it again: *"Now to the King eternal, immortal, invisible, to God who alone is wise, be honor and glory forever and ever. Amen."* The Greek word that is here translated *"invisible"* means, in this context, not only what is unseen but what is *unseeable.* God, in His inmost essence, in His real personality, is unseeable.

Does it follow, then, that God has no body or form at all? Not by any means. You and I in our real selves are unseeable. These bodies that we inhabit and that men see are not our real selves. No one has ever really seen *me*, except as I reveal myself by a smile or a frown or by a particular look in my eyes or by the cast of my countenance, all of which I form by my temperament and conduct. This body that people see is only the house I live in; it is not I. If the Lord tarries and I pass through the experience of what men call "death," it will not be I who die and crumble into dust; it will be only this house I live in, my *"earthly house, this tent,"* as the apostle Paul put it in 2 Corinthians 5:1. I, my real self, will depart to be with Christ in conscious blessedness (Phil. 1:23). When the Lord Jesus comes again, my body will be raised from the dust (Dan. 12:2; 1 Thess. 4:16) and transformed into the likeness of *"His glorious body"* (Phil. 3:21). Even that body will not be my real self but my *"habitation,"* my *"habitation which is from heaven"* (2 Cor. 5:2).

When Jesus was crucified and died, His *body* was laid in Joseph's tomb and kept from decay, but *He Himself*, bodiless, went into Hades. That is what Peter said on the Day of Pentecost. Read his words: "[David], *foreseeing this* [that the Christ would come from his lineage], *spoke concerning the resurrection of the Christ, that His soul was not left in Hades, nor did His flesh see corruption"* (Acts 2:31). Here a clear-cut distinction is drawn between *"His soul,"* Jesus Himself, who went into Hades, and *"His flesh"* (or body), which went into Joseph's tomb and no further. So we come back to the original question, Does God have a body, a visible form, in which He manifests Himself?

Spirit Manifests Itself Visibly

In reply to this question, let me say, first of all, that the Bible clearly teaches that what is Spirit manifests itself in visible form. We see in John 1:32 that John the Baptist said, *"I saw the Spirit descending from heaven like a dove."* Here not only *a* spirit but *"the Spirit"* was seen in visible form. The Greek word translated *"saw"* is a very strong word for seeing with the physical eye.

Jehovah God Manifested Himself in Visible Form

Second, in Exodus 24:9–10, we are told that Jehovah, the God of Israel, manifested Himself in visible form and was seen. Let us look at this passage:

> *Then Moses went up, also Aaron, Nadab, and Abihu, and seventy of the elders of Israel, and they saw the God of Israel. And there was under His feet as it were a paved work of sapphire stone, and it was like the very heavens in its clarity.*

What was seen in these visible manifestations of God? The answer is plain: what was seen was not God Himself, that is, God in His invisible essence, but merely a visible manifestation of God. This point is clear from John 1:18: *"No one has seen God at any time. The only begotten Son, who is in the bosom of the Father, He has declared Him."* It is also clear from the book of Exodus itself. We read in Exodus 33:18–23:

> *And [Moses] said, "Please, show me Your glory." Then [God] said, "I will make all My goodness pass before you, and I will proclaim the name of the LORD before you. I will be gracious to whom I will be gracious, and I will*

have compassion on whom I will have compassion." But He said, "You cannot see My face; for no man shall see Me, and live." And the LORD said, "Here is a place by Me, and you shall stand on the rock. So it shall be, while My glory passes by, that I will put you in the cleft of the rock, and will cover you with My hand while I pass by. Then I will take away My hand, and you shall see My back; but My face shall not be seen." (Exod. 33:18–23)

Many people are greatly perplexed by the apparent contradiction between John 1:18, *"No one has seen God at any time,"* and Exodus 24:9–10, *"Then Moses went up, also Aaron, Nadab, and Abihu, and seventy of the elders of Israel, and they saw the God of Israel."* But when one stops to think it through, he sees that there is really no contradiction at all. It is perfectly true that *"No one has seen God"*—that is, God Himself, God as He is in His invisible essence—*"at any time."* God, in His essence, in His inmost personality, is unseeable. For that matter, as I said earlier, no one has even seen R. A. Torrey at any time. People have seen this body that I live in, but have they seen me? I think not. Do you think that people know me? I think not. One of my misfortunes is that my face and eyes reveal so little of what I feel in my heart. Sometimes, perhaps, it is my good fortune that this is so. In any event, men *have seen God;* that is, they have seen the form in which He has manifested Himself—for example, the form in which He manifested Himself to the seventy elders on Mt. Sinai.

Therefore, two statements that appear to flatly contradict one another may both be perfectly true.

Here is an illustration of this point: A man may see the reflection of the back of his head in a mirror. It would be perfectly true for that man to say, "I saw the back of my head in the mirror." But it would also be true for him to say, "I have never seen the back of my head." What he really saw was not the back of his head; it was only a reflection of the back of his head in a mirror. To be still more exact, no one has ever seen the back of anyone's head. When we say, with perfect truthfulness, "I saw the back of a man's head," what we have really seen is the reflection of the back of that man's head on the retina of our eye. In the same way, a few men have seen a manifestation of God, and it is perfectly true to say that these men *saw God*. But no man has ever seen God as He is in His invisible essence, the true God Himself; therefore, it is perfectly true to say, *"No one has seen God at any time."*

The Angel of the Lord Was a Visible Manifestation of God

Third, the Angel of the Lord in the Old Testament, who frequently appeared and was seen by Abraham, Manoah, and others, was a Divine Person, God in human form. A clear distinction is drawn in the Bible between *an* angel of the Lord and *the* Angel of the Lord. The King James Version does not always preserve the distinction; the American Standard Edition of the Revised Version and other versions, following the Hebrew text of the Old Testament and the Greek text of the New Testament, always do. That the Angel of the Lord is a Divine Person is perfectly clear from many passages. Read, for example, Genesis 16:7–10:

Now the Angel of the LORD found [Hagar] *by a spring of water in the wilderness, by the*

*spring on the way to Shur. And He said, "Ha-
gar, Sarai's maid, where have you come from,
and where are you going?" She said, "I am
fleeing from the presence of my mistress
Sarai." The Angel of the LORD said to her,
"Return to your mistress, and submit yourself
under her hand." Then the Angel of the LORD
said to her, "I will multiply your descendants
exceedingly, so that they shall not be counted
for multitude."* (Gen. 16:7–10)

"The Angel of the LORD" in verse ten is clearly
identified with Jehovah Himself in verse thirteen,
where we are told that Hagar *"called the name of the
LORD who spoke to her, You-Are-the-God-Who-Sees."*
Now, we are told in the preceding verses that the
One who *"spoke to her"* was *"the Angel of the
LORD."* Therefore, the Lord Jehovah and the Angel
of the Lord are clearly identified with one another.

Now let us now read Genesis 21:17–18:

And God heard the voice of the lad [Ishmael].
*Then the angel of God called to Hagar out of
heaven, and said to her, "What ails you, Hagar? Fear not, for God has heard the voice of
the lad where he is. Arise, lift up the lad and
hold him with your hand, for I will make him
a great nation."*

Here it is definitely said that *"the angel of God"*
declared that he would do what only God can do;
therefore, *"the angel of God"* is distinctly described
as a Divine Person.

Judges 2:1–2 gives us another illustration of
this:

> *Then the Angel of the LORD came up from Gilgal to Bochim, and said: "I led you up from Egypt and brought you to the land of which I swore to your fathers; and I said, 'I will never break My covenant with you. And you shall make no covenant with the inhabitants of this land; you shall tear down their altars.' But you have not obeyed My voice. Why have you done this?"*
> *(Judg. 2:1–2)*

Here *"the Angel of the LORD"* distinctly said that it was he who brought the Israelites up out of Egypt, that it was he who promised the land to their fathers, and that it was he who made a covenant with Israel. Now, it was certainly Jehovah who did all these things, and therefore it is as clear as day that *"the Angel of the LORD"* is identified with Jehovah Himself.

A very noteworthy passage in this connection is Genesis 18. Let us look at various verses from that chapter:

> *Then the LORD appeared to him* [Abraham] *by the terebinth trees of Mamre, as he was sitting in the tent door in the heat of the day. So he lifted his eyes and looked, and behold, three men were standing by him* [evidently, one of the three who appeared as *"three men"* was the LORD, for it says in verse one that *"the LORD appeared to him"*]; *and when he saw them, he ran from the tent door to meet them, and bowed himself to the ground....Then they said to him, "Where is Sarah your wife?" So he said, "Here, in the tent." And He* [that is, one of the three] *said, "I will certainly return*

*to you according to the time of life, and behold,
Sarah your wife shall have a son." (Sarah was
listening in the tent door which was behind
him.)...And the LORD said* [here it says distinctly that it was *"the LORD"* who said what
one of the three men said] *to Abraham, "Why
did Sarah laugh, saying, 'Shall I surely bear a
child, since I am old?' Is anything too hard for
the LORD? At the appointed time I will return
to you, according to the time of life, and Sarah
shall have a son."...Then the men rose from
there and looked toward Sodom, and Abraham went with them to send them on the way.*
(Gen. 18:1–2, 9–10, 13–14, 16)

Here we see once more that one of these three
persons who appeared in human form is identified
again and again with Jehovah. Now let us go to the
nineteenth chapter of Genesis. We read in the first
verse that only two of the three who talked to Abraham entered Sodom in the evening. Here are the
words: *"Now the two angels came to Sodom in the
evening, and Lot was sitting in the gate of Sodom."*
One of the three, therefore, remained behind, and
two went on. Who was the one who remained behind? It is perfectly clear as we read this prior passage from the eighteenth chapter of Genesis:

And the LORD said [it is evident, then, that
the Lord was the One of the three who remained behind], *"Shall I hide from Abraham
what I am doing, since Abraham shall surely
become a great and mighty nation, and all the
nations of the earth shall be blessed in him?
For I have known him, in order that he may*

*command his children and his household after
him, that they keep the way of the LORD, to do
righteousness and justice, that the LORD may
bring to Abraham what He has spoken to
him." And the LORD said, "Because the outcry
against Sodom and Gomorrah is great, and
because their sin is very grave, **I will go down
now** and see whether they have done altogether
according to the outcry against it that has
come to Me; and if not, I will know."*

(Gen. 18:17–21, emphasis added)

We read next in verse twenty-two that *"the men
turned away from there and went toward Sodom*
[that is, the two men, for only two entered Sodom, as
we saw in Genesis 19:1], *but Abraham still stood before the LORD."* Clearly, then, the One of the three
who remained behind was Jehovah manifested in
the form of a man. In verse thirty-three of chapter
eighteen, the story continues: *"So the LORD went
His way as soon as He had finished speaking with
Abraham; and Abraham returned to his place."* And
in the twenty-seventh verse of the nineteenth chapter, we read: *"And Abraham went early in the morning to the place where he had stood before the LORD."*
So there is no room left to question that the One
who remained behind while the other two went on to
Sodom, the One before whom Abraham *"had stood,"*
was Jehovah appearing in human form.

In Zechariah 12:8, we find a very clear statement of the fact that *"the Angel of the LORD"* is a
Divine Person. This is how it reads:

*In that day the LORD will defend the inhabi-
tants of Jerusalem; the one who is feeble*

*among them in that day shall be like David,
and the house of David shall be like God, like
the Angel of the LORD before them. (Zech. 12:8)*

Here *"the Angel of the LORD"* is distinctly stated to be *"God."*

In all these passages, *"the Angel of the LORD"* is clearly identified with Jehovah Himself; that is, He is the visible manifestation of Jehovah. Just who was, then, *"the Angel of the LORD"*? This becomes perfectly clear by a comparison of a passage in the book of Judges with the prophecy concerning the coming Messiah in Isaiah 9.

In Judges 13:18, we read: *"And the Angel of the LORD said to [Manoah], 'Why do you ask My name, seeing it is wonderful?'"* The King James Version translates the phrase as *"seeing it is secret,"* but this is beyond question an incorrect translation. Now let us turn to Isaiah 9:6–7, where we are told that the name of the coming Messiah, who would be a Divine Person, is *"Wonderful"*:

For unto us a Child is born, unto us a Son is given; and the government will be upon His shoulder. And His name will be called Wonderful, Counselor, Mighty God, Everlasting Father, Prince of Peace. Of the increase of His government and peace there will be no end, upon the throne of David and over His kingdom, to order it and establish it with judgment and justice from that time forward, even forever.

Here we see that it is the Messiah whose name is to be called *"Wonderful,"* but the passage in Judges says that the name of *"the Angel of the LORD"* is *"wonderful."* The Hebrew word that is translated *"wonderful"* in Judges 13:18 is almost identical to the word used in Isaiah, except that in the first case it is an adjective and in the second case it is the noun from which that adjective is derived.

From these Scripture texts, it is clear that the Angel of the Lord of the Old Testament was the Son of God before His permanent incarnation in the person of Jesus of Nazareth. This throws much light upon what we read in John 1:1–3, 14:

> *In the beginning was the Word, and the Word was with God, and the Word was God. He was in the beginning with God. All things were made through Him, and without Him nothing was made that was made....And the Word became flesh and dwelt among us, and we beheld His glory, the glory as of the only begotten of the Father, full of grace and truth.*

It should be added that the Angel of the Lord never appears in Scripture after the birth of Jesus, the Christ. The expression does occur in the King James Version, but in every instance, it is a mistranslation, as is clear from the American Standard Edition of the Revised Version and other versions. In every such case, these versions translate the term as *"**an** angel of the Lord,"* just as the Greek text reads, instead of *"**the** angel of the Lord,"* used in the King James Version.

Our Lord Jesus Himself referred to these previous manifestations of Himself in human form in John 8:56, where He said, *"Your father Abraham rejoiced to see My day, and he saw it and was glad."* It was in seeing our Lord Jesus at Mamre in the Angel of the Lord (Genesis 18) that Abraham "saw" Jesus' day.

God Existed in Visible Form from Eternity

But this is not all that can be said about God having a body or form. In the fourth place, the Bible clearly teaches that God existed, even before His incarnation in the person of Jesus of Nazareth, in a visible form in the eternal world. This we see from a comparison of John 1:1–3, 14, which we read in the last section, with Philippians 2:5–6, where we read: *"Have this mind in you, which was also in Christ Jesus: who, existing in the form of God"* (ASV). The word translated *"existing"* in the American Standard Edition of the Revised Version is a rather unusual and very remarkable word. It means "existing substantially" or "being originally" (RV, margin). The word translated *"form,"* according to *Thayer's Greek-English Lexicon of the New Testament*, means, in Greek usage (and has from the time of Homer), "the form by which a person or thing strikes the vision; the external appearance." But we are told that the form in which the Divine Person who became incarnate in the person of Jesus of Nazareth existed originally was *"the form of God."* (See Philippians 2:6, 9–10.) Therefore, God must have a *"form."* It is clear, then, that although *"God is* [essentially] *Spirit"* (John 4:24), nevertheless He has a form in which He is seen.

The Form of God Is Seen in Heaven

Fifth, the fact that Jehovah manifests Himself in a form may be clearly seen in Acts 7:55–56:

> *But* [Stephen], *being full of the Holy Spirit,*
> *gazed into heaven and saw the glory of God,*
> *and Jesus standing at the right hand of God,*
> *and said, "Look! I see the heavens opened and*
> *the Son of Man standing at the right hand of*
> *God!"*   (*Acts 7:55–56*)

Since Stephen saw Jesus *"standing at the right hand of God,"* he must have seen God at whose right hand he saw Jesus standing.

All that has been said on this point may be summed up in this way: God, in His essential personality, is Spirit—invisible, incorporeal, unseeable. However, He has a form in which He manifests Himself in the heavenly world and is seen.

Therefore, Matthew 5:8, *"Blessed are the pure in heart, for they shall see God,"* is true not only of a spiritual vision of God but of an actual, visible, bodily seeing of God, God in a visible form. Such a vision of God is so glorious that we could not see Him in this way in our present mortal bodies and live. Jehovah said to Moses in Exodus 33:20, *"You cannot see My face; for no man shall see Me, and live."* What deep significance this gives to Psalm 17:15 (as correctly rendered in the American Standard Edition of the Revised Version): *"As for me, I shall behold thy face in righteousness; I shall be satisfied, when I awake,* ***with beholding thy form"*** (ASV, emphasis added). (For a deeper study of the usage and meaning of the Hebrew word here translated *"form,"* compare the following verses in the Hebrew: Numbers 12:8, Job 4:16, and Deuteronomy 4:12, 15.)

It also gives new meaning to those wonderful words of our Lord in John 14:9, *"He who has seen*

Me has seen the Father." In the person of Jesus in His humiliation, when He had put off for the time being the divine form (see Philippians 2:6–7), men saw God as *"in a mirror, dimly"* (1 Cor. 13:12), that is, in an enigma. But in that coming Day when, having resumed the divine form, He comes back again, in Him we will see God fully revealed—*"face to face"* (v. 12). We will see God in His full and un-dimmed glory. That is the highest joy that man is capable of knowing.

Chapter 3

GOD IS ONE IN
THREE PERSONS

The grace of the Lord Jesus Christ, and the love of
God, and the communion of the Holy Spirit
be with you all.
—2 Corinthians 13:14

The Scripture passages we will be looking at in this chapter prove beyond a doubt that, according to the Bible, there is only one God. They also contain a definite and clear answer to the question, Are there three Persons in this one God? Let us begin by looking at some Scripture texts that will illuminate our understanding of this question:

Hear, O Israel: the LORD our God, the LORD is
one! You shall love the LORD your God with
all your heart, with all your soul, and with all
your strength. *(Deut. 6:4–5)*

Let Us make man in Our image, according to
Our likeness. *(Gen. 1:26)*

From [the Israelites], *according to the flesh, Christ came, who is over all, the eternally blessed God. Amen.* (*Rom. 9:5*)

In the beginning was the Word, and the Word was with God, and the Word was God. He was in the beginning with God. All things were made through Him, and without Him nothing was made that was made....And the Word became flesh and dwelt among us, and we beheld His glory, the glory as of the only begotten of the Father, full of grace and truth.

(*John 1:1–3, 14*)

The grace of the Lord Jesus Christ, and the love of God, and the communion of the Holy Spirit be with you all. (*2 Cor. 13:14*)

THERE IS ONLY ONE GOD

The first fact about God that our texts teach is that there is only one God. This is the great foundational truth of the Bible from the very first verse in it—"*In the beginning God created the heavens and the earth*"—to the close of the last book in it—"*I am the Alpha and the Omega, the Beginning and the End, the First and the Last*" (Rev. 22:13). Intelligent Israelites have always considered Deuteronomy 6:4–5—"*Hear, O Israel: the LORD our God, the LORD is one! You shall love the LORD your God with all your heart, with all your soul, and with all your strength*" —as the very heart of the revelation made by God to them through Moses and the prophets of the old dispensation. (By "old dispensation," I mean the way God related to man before the new covenant in

52

Christ.) Moreover, our Lord Jesus Himself endorsed this view by saying in answer to a question that was asked Him by one of the scribes—*"Which is the first commandment of all?"* (Mark 12:28)—

> *The first of all the commandments is: "Hear, O Israel, the LORD our God, the LORD is one. And you shall love the LORD your God with all your heart, with all your soul, with all your mind, and with all your strength." This is the first commandment.* (vv. 29–30)

The teaching of the Bible has no tolerance for polytheism in any form. It is monotheistic from start to finish. In this respect, the God of the Bible differs from the god of Theosophy. Theosophy is simply Buddhism in a new guise, and not a very new guise at that. Buddhism is polytheism gone mad. It has literally millions of gods. And when you get to the heart of Theosophy, you find that it has a multitude of what are really gods. Indeed, when you get to the very heart of Theosophy, it says that we are all gods (except when Theosophy assumes a pantheistic form, in which case we are *all* God, and there is no God except us and everything else).

The same thing is true of Christian Science. Christian Science is always essentially pantheistic or polytheistic or a combination of both pantheism and polytheism. At the heart of Christian Science is the thought that we are all gods. According to Christian Science, as stated in Mrs. Eddy's book, *Science and Health*, it is not only "God is Spirit," but "Spirit is God," and we are all essentially and only spirit. To think that we have bodies is "illusion" or "mortal thought"; therefore, we are all gods. According to Christian Science, think that you are God, and you are God. Here are some other excerpts from *Science and Health* that illustrate this point and show how the true meaning of the Bible is distorted in the teachings of Christian Science:

Question: What is God?
Answer: God is Divine principle, Supreme, Incorporeal Being, Mind, Spirit, Soul, Life, Truth, Love.
Question: Are these terms synonymous?
Answer: They are; they refer to one absolute God and nothing else. They are also intended to express the nature, essence, and holiness of Deity.

Question: What are spirits and souls?
Answer: To human belief they are personalities constituted of Mind and matter, Life and death, Truth and error, Good and evil; but these contrasting pairs of terms represent opposites, as Christian Science reveals—neither dwelling together nor assimilating.

The term *souls* or *spirits* is as improper as the term *gods*. Soul, or Spirit, signifies Deity and nothing else. There is no finite soul or spirit. These terms mean only one Mind, and cannot be rendered in the plural. Heathen mythology and Jewish theology have perpetuated the fallacy that intelligence, soul, and life can be in matter; and idolatry and ritualism are the outcome of these man-made beliefs. The Science of Christianity comes with fan in hand, to separate the chaff from the wheat.

Question: What is the science of soul?
Answer: The first demand of this science is, "Thou shall have no other gods before me." This me is spirit.

God Is One in Three Persons

It should be well understood that all men have one Mind, one God and Father, one Life, Truth, and Love.

Having no other gods, turning to no other mind but the one perfect Intelligence to guide him, man is the likeness of God, pure and eternal, having that mind which was also in Christ Jesus.

We lose the high significance of omnipotence, when admitting that God, or good, is omnipresent, and has all-power, yet that there is another power named evil. This belief, that there is more than one mind, is as pernicious to divine theology as our ancient mythology and pagan idolatry....The existence of more than one mind was the basic error of idolatry.

To quote once more from Mrs. Eddy in *Science and Health*, "Spirit cannot believe in God. Spirit is God." The necessary corollary of this is that insofar as you and I are spirit, you and I are God. And it is the constant teaching of Mrs. Eddy that, in pure Christian Science, you and I are only spirit, and it is only due to "mortal thought" or "error" that we have bodies at all. Therefore, every one of us, in the ultimate thought of Christian Science, is God.

What I have said of Theosophy and Christian Science, namely, that they are essentially polytheistic or pantheistic, is also true of much of the so-called New Theology and of a very large share of modern philosophy. George Albert Coe, professor at Union Theological Seminary in New York, wrote in *Religious Education*:

I worship the God, who breathing himself everywhere into the human clod, makes it a spirit, a social craving, even the spirit of humanity, yes, the spirit of a possible world society.

55

Take careful note of this next statement. Professor Coe also wrote, "I bow my spirit before the spirit of the world democracy that is to be."

The Reverend R. J. Campbell, the former leader and high priest of New Theology, said in a sermon,

> Sin is a quest for God—a blundering quest, but a quest for all that. The man who got dead drunk last night did so because of the impulse within him to break through the barriers of his limitations, to express himself, and to realize the more abundant life. His self-indulgence just came to that; he wanted, if only for a brief hour, to live the larger life, to expand the soul, to enter untrodden regions, and gather to himself new experiences. That drunken debauch was a quest for light, a quest for God. Men who in their sinful follies today, their trampling upon things that are beautiful and good, are engaged in this dim, blundering quest for God, whom to know is life eternal.

The inescapable inference from these shocking words is that everything in us, even our sinful propensities, is divine. However, it would not be fair to attribute such an idea of the essential divinity of man at his worst to all New Theology men. R. J. Campbell's statement represents New Theology on a drunken binge, or New Theology gone stark crazy. But, after all, this is really the logical outcome of the fundamental principles of Modernistic thinking and of the thinking of much that passes for modern scholarship and modern philosophy. We need the apostle Paul's warning today as much as the saints in Colosse needed it:

Beware lest anyone cheat you through philoso-
phy and empty deceit, according to the tradi-
tion of men, according to the basic principles
of the world, and not according to Christ.
(Col. 2:8)

But in the Bible, the thought that there is a personal God, separate and distinct from all the things
and persons that He has created, and that there is
only one God, dominates the whole Book, both the
Old Testament and the New. Consider these verses:

To you it was shown, that you might know
that the LORD Himself is God; there is none
other besides Him.   (Deut. 4:35)

"You are My witnesses," says the LORD, "and
My servant whom I have chosen, that you may
know and believe Me, and understand that I
am He. Before Me there was no God formed,
nor shall there be after Me. I, even I, am the
LORD, and besides Me there is no savior."
(Isa. 43:10–11)

Thus says the LORD, the King of Israel, and
his Redeemer, the LORD of hosts: "I am the
First and I am the Last; besides Me there is no
God."   (Isa. 44:6)

I am the LORD, and there is no other; there is
no God besides Me.   (Isa. 45:5)

Jesus answered him, "The first of all the
commandments is: 'Hear, O Israel, the LORD
our God, the LORD is one. And you shall love

*the LORD your God with all your heart, with
all your soul, with all your mind, and with all
your strength.' This is the first commandment."*   (Mark 12:29–30)

*There is one God and one Mediator between
God and men, the Man Christ Jesus.*
                                        (1 Tim. 2:5)

Finally, let us look at what our Lord Jesus Himself said to the rich young man who came to Him
kneeling and calling Him *"good"* (Mark 10:17). This
young man did not understand the deeper meaning
in his own .words, which were profoundly true although he did not grasp the truth of them, and
which our Lord desired that he should grasp. Jesus
said to him, *"Why do you call Me good? No one is
good but One, that is, God"* (v. 18).

That there is one God and only one God is the
great foundational rock of the entire Bible—in New
Testament thought as well as Old Testament
thought.

ARE THERE THREE PERSONS IN THE ONE GOD?

We come now to the second point of consideration, which is tremendously important: Are there
three Persons in the one God? Many conclude, because it is so plainly and so constantly taught in the
Bible that there is only one God, that God the Father is all that there is of the one God and that,
therefore, Jesus Christ cannot be God and the Holy
Spirit cannot be God. This is the fundamental con-
tention of both orthodox and liberal Jewish theology.

Also, it was this thought that gave rise to modern Unitarianism.

Does it follow that, because there is only one God, Jesus Christ cannot be God and the Holy Spirit cannot be God? No. We will see by the teachings of the whole Bible, by the teachings of the Old Testament as clearly as by the teachings of the New Testament, that there are three Divine Persons in the one Godhead.

A Compound Unity

In the first place, the Hebrew word translated *"one"* in Deuteronomy 6:4–5, which I have quoted as conclusively proving that there is only one God, denotes a compound unity and not a simple unity. Let me illustrate this truth using several Scripture passages. In Genesis 2:24, we read: *"Therefore a man shall leave his father and mother and be joined to his wife, and they shall become one flesh."* Now the Hebrew word translated *"one"* in this passage is the same word that is translated *"one"* in the various passages that declare that there is only "one God." It can be plainly seen in this passage that not a simple unity but a compound unity is intended, that is, two—man and wife—being *"one."*

Let us turn now to Genesis 11:6: *"And the LORD said, 'Indeed the people are one.'"* The same Hebrew word for "one" is used here. In this verse, we are told that a large number of people are one people; they are at the same time many and one. We find a similar usage of the Greek word for "one" in the New Testament. For example, let us look at 1 Corinthians 3:6–8:

> *I planted, Apollos watered, but God gave the
> increase. So then neither he who plants is any-
> thing, nor he who waters, but God who gives
> the increase. Now he who plants and he who
> waters are one.*   *(1 Cor. 3:6–8)*

Here we are distinctly told that two different persons are *"one."* Next, let us turn to 1 Corinthians
12:13: *"For by one Spirit we were all baptized into
one body; whether Jews or Greeks, whether slaves or
free; and have all been made to drink into one
Spirit."* In this verse, we are distinctly told that all
who have become members of the living church by
the baptism in the Holy Spirit are—together—
"one." In the same way, we read in Galatians 3:28:
*"There is neither Jew nor Greek, there is neither
slave nor free, there is neither male nor female; for
you are all one in Christ Jesus."* Here we find a large
number of people constituting one person.

The Name "God" Is Plural in Its Form

Second, the Old Testament Hebrew word most
frequently used as the name (or title) of God, the
word translated *"God"* many hundreds of times in the
Old Testament, is plural in its form. Literally translated, the word would read "Gods." For example, if we
literally translated one of our texts for this chapter,
Deuteronomy 6:4, it would read, "Hear, O Israel: the
LORD our *Gods*, the LORD is one!"

Yet this is the passage that the Unitarians and
non-Christian Jews so emphasize and insist upon to
disprove the divinity of Christ. Why is it, therefore,
that the Jews, with their intense monotheism, had a

plural name for God? That was the difficult problem that puzzled the ancient Hebrew lexicographers and grammarians. The best answer that they could give was that the plural form used for the name or title of God was the "pluralis majestatis," that is, the plural of majesty (as in the use of *we* in place of *I* in the speech of royalty). In other words, they concluded that a plural name was used for God because of the majesty of His person. Now, to say nothing of the fact that it is not at all certain that the "pluralis majestatis" is ever found in the Old Testament, there is an explanation much nearer at hand and much simpler: a plural name was used for the one God, in spite of the intense monotheism of the Jews, because there *is* a plurality of Persons in the one Godhead. This is a rational explanation for this unquestionable fact; no other explanation is as rational.

God Uses Plural Pronouns in Speaking of Himself

Third, in the Old Testament, God uses plural pronouns in speaking of Himself. He does this in the very first chapter of the Bible, in Genesis 1:26, where it is written, *"Then God said, 'Let Us make man in Our image, according to Our likeness.'"* It is often said that the doctrine of the Trinity is found in the New Testament but not in the Old Testament; however, here we find it in the first chapter of the Old Testament. Indeed, the three Persons of the Trinity are found in the first three verses of the Old Testament:

> *In the beginning God* [here we have God the Father] *created the heavens and the earth. The*

61

> *earth was without form, and void; and dark-*
> *ness was on the face of the deep. And the Spirit*
> *of God* [here we have the Holy Spirit] *was*
> *hovering over the face of the waters. Then God*
> *said* [here we have the Word of God, the Word
> who became incarnate in the person of Jesus
> of Nazareth (see John 1:1–3, 14)], *"Let there*
> *be light"; and there was light.*   (Gen. 1:1–3)

It is an interesting and indicative fact, although
I do not know that there is really anything to it, that
the first three letters in the Hebrew Bible are the
initials of the Father, Son, and Holy Spirit. The first
letter in the Hebrew Bible is the Hebrew equivalent
of the letter *b*, which is the initial of the Hebrew
word *ben*, which signifies "son." The second letter of
the Hebrew Bible is the Hebrew equivalent of the
letter *r*, which is the initial of the Hebrew word *ru-*
wach, which means "spirit." And the third letter of
the Hebrew Bible is the Hebrew equivalent of the
letter *a*, which is the initial of the Hebrew word *ab*,
which means "father." Whether there is any significance in this fact or not, it is certainly true that the
three Persons of the Trinity are in the first three
verses of the Old Testament, and that in Genesis
1:26, the plurality of Persons in the Godhead is distinctly taught.

We see this plurality again in the vision of God
that Jehovah gave to the prophet Isaiah. In Isaiah
6:8, we read: *"Also I heard the voice of the Lord, say-*
ing: 'Whom shall I send, and who will go for Us?'"

These are not the only instances in which Jehovah is depicted in the Old Testament as using plural
pronouns in speaking of Himself, but these are sufficient to prove the point.

There is another suggestion of the tri-personality
of God earlier in the sixth chapter of Isaiah:

*In the year that King Uzziah died, I saw the
Lord sitting on a throne, high and lifted up,
and the train of His robe filled the temple.
Above it stood seraphim; each one had six
wings: with two he covered his face, with two
he covered his feet, and with two he flew. And
one cried to another and said: "Holy, holy,
holy is the LORD of hosts; the whole earth is
full of His glory!"* (Isa. 6:1–3)

Is there not in this threefold *"holy,"* and especially when taken in connection with verse eight, a
suggestion of the tri-personality of *"the LORD of
hosts"*? Furthermore, this vision is referred to in the
New Testament. In one place where it is referred to,
John 12:37–41, it is said that Isaiah spoke the words
that he is recorded as speaking in Isaiah 6, when he
saw the glory of the Lord Jesus and spoke of Him.
"These things Isaiah said when he saw [Jesus'] *glory
and spoke of Him"* (John 12:41). Yet in the passage
in Isaiah, we are distinctly told that it was the
Lord's glory that Isaiah saw. Moreover, in another
place in the New Testament where this same vision
of Isaiah is referred to, we are distinctly told that it
was the Holy Spirit who said what Jehovah is recorded to have said. (See Acts 28:25–27.)

The Lord Speaks of Himself as Sent by the Lord

Fourth, in Zechariah 2:10–11, the Lord speaks of
Himself as sent by the Lord, thus clearly implying at

least two distinct Persons in the one God Jehovah. Let us look at this passage:

> *"Sing and rejoice, O daughter of Zion! For behold, I am coming and I will dwell in your midst," says the LORD. "Many nations shall be joined to the LORD in that day, and they shall become My people. And I will dwell in your midst. Then you will know that the LORD of hosts has sent Me to you."*   *(Zech. 2:10–11)*

Here we have Jehovah, the Lord, as both the One sending and the One sent. (See also John 8:29; 14:24.)

The Angel of the Lord Is both Jehovah and the Christ

Fifth, we saw in the preceding chapter that the Angel of the Lord was both identified with Jehovah and distinguished from Him, and we saw by a comparison of Judges 13:18 with Isaiah 9:6–7 that, beyond question, the Angel of the Lord was that Person of the Godhead who afterwards became incarnate in the Messiah.

"The Word Was with God, and...Was God."

Sixth, we are distinctly told in John 1:1–3, 14 that the eternal Word of God who afterward became incarnate in Jesus of Nazareth *"was with God"* and *"was* [Himself] *God."* You are probably perfectly familiar with the words, but let us read them again:

> *In the beginning was the Word, and the Word was with God, and the Word was God. He was in the beginning with God. All things were*

made through Him, and without Him nothing
was made that was made....And the Word be-
came flesh and dwelt among us, and we beheld
His glory, the glory as of the only begotten of
the Father, full of grace and truth.

Jesus and the Holy Spirit Are Set Forth as Divine Persons

Seventh, both Jesus Christ, the Son of God, and
the Holy Spirit are clearly set forth in the New Testament as Divine Persons. I could show you this
truth in many ways and by a multitude of passages,
which would take many pages to present and ade-
quately expound upon. Let two of our texts for this
chapter and two other passages suffice:

Of whom [the Israelites] *are the fathers and*
from whom, according to the flesh, Christ
came, who is over all, the eternally blessed
God.   *(Rom. 9:5)*

Thomas answered and said to [Jesus], *"My*
Lord and my God!" Jesus said to him, "Tho-
mas, because you have seen Me, you have be-
lieved. Blessed are those who have not seen
and yet have believed."   *(John 20:28–29)*

The grace of the Lord Jesus Christ, and the
love of God, and the communion of the Holy
Spirit be with you all.   *(2 Cor. 13:14)*

Peter said, "Ananias, why has Satan filled your
heart to lie to the Holy Spirit and keep back part
of the price of the land for yourself? While it
remained, was it not your own? And after it
was sold, was it not in your own control? Why

have you conceived this thing in your heart?
You have not lied to men but to God."

(Acts 5:3–4)

In Acts 5:3, Peter distinctly said that Ananias lied to the Holy Spirit, and in Acts 5:4, he just as distinctly said that Ananias lied to God, thus clearly teaching that the Holy Spirit is God.

The Messiah Is Depicted as a Divine Person

Eighth, the Old Testament clearly declares the predicted Messiah to be a Divine Person, just as clearly as the New Testament declares the historical Christ, Christ Jesus, to be a Divine Person. Let me give you a few Scripture passages as examples. First of all, let us look at Micah 5:2:

> *But you, Bethlehem Ephrathah, though you are little among the thousands of Judah, yet out of you shall come forth to Me the One to be Ruler in Israel, whose goings forth are from of old, from everlasting.*

In this prophecy, the coming Messiah is distinctly depicted as a Person who has existed eternally. Let us now read Isaiah 9:6–7:

> *For unto us a Child is born, unto us a Son is given; and the government will be upon His shoulder. And His name will be called Wonderful, Counselor, Mighty God, Everlasting Father, Prince of Peace. Of the increase of His government and peace there will be no end, upon the throne of David and over His kingdom, to order it and establish it with judgment and justice from that time forward, even forever.*

There are at least three unmistakably divine names attributed to the coming Messiah in this wonderful prophecy, one of those divine names being *"Mighty God."*

Isaac Leeser, in his translation of the Hebrew Bible into English, has inserted four words into this verse for which there are no equivalent words whatsoever in the Hebrew text. He inserted them for the specific purpose of obscuring the significance of the passage's clear declaration that the Messiah was to be a Divine Person. He put the preposition *of* and the definite article *the* before *"Mighty God"* in order to make it read, "Counselor of the Mighty God," and he inserted the same two words before *"Everlasting Father."* As I said, there are no equivalent words whatsoever for these four words in the Hebrew text. Leeser knew this, for he himself did not insert *of* before *"Prince of Peace,"* and there is just as much reason for inserting it there as before *"Mighty God"* or *"Everlasting Father."*

In the ecclesiastically authorized translation of the Hebrew Bible into English, authorized by the Jewish authorities, the meaning that is so plain in this verse is concealed. In this version, the names are not translated at all but are transliterated from the Hebrew. However, there can be no doubt about it, to any honest student of the Hebrew Bible, that at least three distinctly divine names are ascribed to the Messiah in this passage.

Let us now look at Jeremiah 23:5–6:

"Behold, the days are coming," says the LORD, "that I will raise to David a Branch of righteousness; a King shall reign and prosper, and

*execute judgment and righteousness in the
earth. In His days Judah will be saved, and
Israel will dwell safely; now this is His name
by which He will be called: THE LORD OUR
RIGHTEOUSNESS."* (Jer. 23:5–6)

In Psalm 45:6–7, one of the unquestionably
messianic psalms, we read these words addressed to
the coming Messiah:

*Your throne, O God, is forever and ever; a
scepter of righteousness is the scepter of Your
kingdom. You love righteousness and hate
wickedness; therefore God, Your God, has
anointed You with the oil of gladness more
than Your companions.*

Here we have the coming Messiah distinctly named
as a Divine Person. He is called *"God,"* yet at the
same time He is distinguished from *"God,"* who
would anoint Him with the Holy Spirit to qualify
Him for His work. It is clear, then, that the Messiah
of the Old Testament was to be a Divine Person,
"God," manifested in a human person, God Incarnate, just as clearly as it is asserted in the Bible that
when the Messiah, Jesus of Nazareth, was born,
lived, died, rose again, and ascended to the right
hand of the Father, He was a Divine Person, God in
human form, God Incarnate.

Six of the eight reasons just given would prove
that in the teaching of the Old Testament as well as
in the teaching of the New Testament there are
three Divine Persons in the one Godhead. But taking
the eight reasons together, there is no possibility of
doubt on the part of anyone who is really trying to

find out what the Bible, in both the Old and New Testaments, teaches. In the one God of the Bible, there are three Persons.

A heretical sect arose in the early history of the church. Those belonging to the sect were called Sabellians after Sabellius, their leader, a philosopher of Egypt in the third century. This sect tried to explain the ascription of deity to the Lord Jesus and to the Holy Spirit and to reconcile this fact with the biblical doctrine that there is only one God. They said that Father, Son, and Holy Spirit are not three distinct Persons but three different ways in which the one Person, God, manifests Himself at different times—sometimes as Father, sometimes as Son, and sometimes as Holy Spirit. In the eighteenth century, the Swedish scientist, philosopher, and religious writer Emanuel Swedenborg adopted this explanation, and it is the doctrine of the Swedenborgian church and of some other heretical churches today. But it will not bear careful examination. For the Bible, while clearly ascribing deity to the Lord Jesus and to the Holy Spirit, just as clearly distinguishes Father, Son, and Holy Spirit from one another. For example, let us look at Matthew 3:16–17:

> *When He had been baptized, Jesus came up immediately from the water; and behold, the heavens were opened to Him, and He saw the Spirit of God descending like a dove and alighting upon Him. And suddenly a voice came from heaven, saying, "This is My beloved Son, in whom I am well pleased."*

Here it is distinctly set before us that Jesus, one Person, was standing in the Jordan River; that the

Father, another Person, spoke to Him out of heaven; and that the Spirit of God, a third Person, was descending from the Father through the air to the Son.

Now let us read Matthew 28:19: *"Go therefore and make disciples of all the nations, baptizing them in the name of the Father and of the Son and of the Holy Spirit."* In this verse, the clearest possible distinction is drawn between the three Persons who are named separately. Our Lord Jesus did not say, "Baptizing them in the name of the Father, Son, and Holy Spirit," as it would be necessary to say if They were simply three manifestations of the one God. Instead, He said, *"Baptizing them in the name of the Father and of the Son and of the Holy Spirit."*

Let us look at one other passage that makes the distinction between the Persons of the Trinity perfectly clear: *"The grace of the Lord Jesus Christ, and the love of God, and the communion of the Holy Spirit be with you all"* (2 Cor. 13:14).

HOW CAN GOD BE THREE AND ONE AT THE SAME TIME?

We come, then, face-to-face with the great question that has divided the church from the earliest centuries: How can God be three and one at the same time? This question caused the great Unitarian controversy that shook all of New England in the days of William Ellery Channing. Channing, a clergyman in the early nineteenth century, was a great thinker, but he went astray in his thinking and led a large section of the New England churches astray. In a similar way, the so-called Modernists have led large sections of the church astray. But even though Channing and his associates were in error, they towered far above all

Modernists in the clarity and depth of their thinking and in the earnestness and honesty of their purpose.

So then, what is the answer to the question, How can God be three and one at the same time? The answer is this: God cannot be and is not three and one *in the same sense*. The Unitarians constantly charge that those who believe in the doctrine of the Trinity make three equal one, but in so asserting, they either do not understand the doctrine of the Trinity or else they deliberately misrepresent it. We do not think that God is three and one in the same sense. In what sense, then, can He be three and one at the same time?

A *perfectly* satisfactory answer to this question is, from the very nature of the case, obviously impossible. The first reason is that, as we saw in the last chapter, God is Spirit, and numbers apply primarily to the physical or material world. Difficulty must always arise when we attempt to comprehend Spiritual Being in the forms of material thought. The second reason is that God is infinite and we are finite. He *"dwell*[s] *in unapproachable light"* (1 Tim. 6:16); therefore, our attempt at a philosophical explanation of the tri-unity of God is an attempt to put the facts of Infinite Being into the forms of finite thought. It is an attempt to put the ocean of truth into the pint-sized cup of human understanding, an attempt that, of necessity, could at the very best be only partially successful.

Furthermore, number has significance only in the realm of the finite. It is a well-known mathematical fact that when you get into the realm of the infinite, finite numbers lose their significance and value. Anyone who has any considerable knowledge of mathematics knows that one divided by infinity

71

equals nothing, and also that three divided by infinity equals nothing. Well then, since things that are equal to the same thing are also equal to one another, it should follow that one as the numerator with infinity as the denominator equals three as the numerator with infinity as the denominator. If you cancel the common denominator, infinity, you have one equals three. Now one does not equal three, but this shows that when you get into the realm of the infinite, finite numbers lose their significance and value.

It does not bother me at all that there is something in the biblical conception of God, the Infinite One, that it is not possible for us to completely grasp with our finite minds. Indeed, if I could completely and thoroughly grasp the conception of God that is given to me in the Bible, I would be bound to doubt that the Bible is a full revelation from the Infinite Mind. The very simplicity of the Unitarian conception of God condemns it. God's Being as well as God's *"judgments"* and God's *"ways"* must be beyond complete *"finding out"* by the finite mind (Rom. 11:33). All the illustrations that men use to attempt to explain the triune nature of God, for example, the illustrations of the three-leaved shamrock or of the tripartite nature of man (spirit, soul, and body), are of no value because they are illustrations taken from the finite in order to illustrate the infinite.

This much we know, that God, in His essence, is one and that, at the same time, He is also three. There is only one God, but this one God makes Himself known to men as Father and Son and Holy Spirit, and these Three are separate personalities. How clearly this fact appears in John 14:16–17, where Jesus says, *"I will pray the Father, and He will give you another Helper, that He may abide with you forever; [even] the Spirit of truth."* Here we distinctly see one Person, the Son, praying to another Person, the Father, and the Father, in answer to the prayer of the Son, sending a third Person, *"another Helper...[even] the Spirit of truth."*

To sum up the biblical conception of the unity of God, there is only one God, eternally existing and manifesting Himself in three Persons—Father, Son, and Holy Spirit. So we can say to the Father, "You are God," and worship Him; and we can say to the Son, our Lord Jesus Christ, as Thomas said to Him, *"My Lord and my God!"* (John 20:28), and worship Him; and we can also address the Holy Spirit as God and worship Him. Together, they are not three Gods but one God. We can worship with the words of the seraphim, *"Holy, holy, holy is the LORD of hosts; the whole earth is full of His glory!"* (Isa. 6:3). And we can sing the Gloria Patri:

> Glory be to the Father, and to the Son, and to
> the Holy Ghost;
> As it was in the beginning, is now, and ever shall
> be, world without end. Amen.

Chapter 4

GOD IS OMNIPRESENT

*"Can anyone hide himself in secret places, so I shall
not see him?" says the LORD; "do I not fill heaven
and earth?" says the LORD.*
—Jeremiah 23:24

Let us review what we have already learned about the nature of God in the last three chapters: (1) the God of the Bible is a personal God; (2) the God of the Bible is, in His essence, Spirit—invisible and incorporeal—but He has manifested Himself to men in a visible form, and He has a form now in which He manifests Himself in the celestial world; and (3) according to the teaching of the Bible, there is only one God; however, in this one God there are three Persons: God the Father, God the Son (Jesus Christ), and God the Holy Spirit.

In this chapter, our topic is: God is omnipresent (everywhere), but is He anywhere in particular? To address this theme, let us begin with three Scripture passages, one taken from the Psalms, one from the Prophets, and one from a New Testament apostle.

Where can I go from Your Spirit? Or where can I flee from Your presence? If I ascend into heaven, You are there; if I make my bed in hell [Sheol, the Hebrew word for *"hell"* here, is equivalent to the Greek word *Haides*, or Hades], *behold, You are there. If I take the wings of the morning, and dwell in the uttermost parts of the sea, even there Your hand shall lead me, and Your right hand shall hold me. If I say, "Surely the darkness shall fall on me," even the night shall be light about me; indeed, the darkness shall not hide from You, but the night shines as the day; the darkness and the light are both alike to You.*

(Ps. 139:7–12)

"Am I a God near at hand," says the LORD, *"and not a God afar off? Can anyone hide himself in secret places, so I shall not see him?"* says the LORD; *"do I not fill heaven and earth?"* says the LORD. (Jer. 23:23–24)

God, who made the world and everything in it, since He is Lord of heaven and earth, does not dwell in temples made with hands. Nor is He worshiped with men's hands, as though He needed anything, since He gives to all life, breath, and all things. And He has made from one blood every nation of men to dwell on all the face of the earth, and has determined their preappointed times and the boundaries of their dwellings, so that they should seek the Lord, in the hope that they might grope for Him and find Him, though He is not far from each one of us; for in Him we live and move and have our being. (Acts 17:24–28)

God Is Omnipresent

It would be difficult to find, outside of the Bible, in all the literature of all nations, ancient or modern, anything comparable in profundity, beauty, and sublimity of thought and expression to these utterances of David, Jeremiah, and Paul, all written so many centuries ago. The passage from Acts was written over eighteen hundred years ago, Jeremiah's prophecy was recorded over twenty-five hundred years ago, and David's psalm was written over twenty-nine hundred years ago. How did the apostle and the prophet and the psalmist attain such majestic conceptions of God so many, many centuries before modern philosophy was even dreamed of? There is only one rational answer to this question, and it is the answer given by the Bible itself: these *"men of God spoke as they were moved* [more literally, "were borne along"] *by the Holy Spirit"* (2 Pet. 1:21). They were inspired by God, and this inspiration extended not only to the concepts (or thoughts) they received, but to the very words in which they expressed these concepts. (See 2 Timothy 3:16; 1 Corinthians 2:13.)

GOD IS EVERYWHERE

The first thing that we notice is plainly and unmistakably taught by all these "God-breathed" (2 Tim. 3:16, literal Greek) passages is that God is everywhere. There is no place that we can go in heaven or in Hades where God is not. As we read in Psalm 139, if we ascend into heaven, God is there; if we descend into Sheol (or Hades—*"the heart of the earth"* [Matt. 12:40]; the abode of all the spirits of the departed up to the time of the resurrection and

77

ascension of our Lord, when the spirits of departed believers were brought to heaven with Christ), God is there. If we go east or west, north or south, to the uttermost parts of land or sea, God is there with us; His own hand leads us, and His right hand holds and protects us.

When I was born sixty-six years ago on the Atlantic coast, God was there by my cradle; now that I live more than three thousand miles away from there on the Pacific coast, He is with me in the lecture room or in my study every day, and He watches by my bed during the hours of the night. He stands beside me unseen but really and personally present as I write these words now. It is wonderful that as I speak to my congregation, my voice is carried by radio hundreds of miles away and people are listening to me there; but that is not as wonderful as the fact that God is there beside them just as He is beside me.

When I was on the other side of the world in the heart of Hunan in China last summer, and there seemed to be danger of robbery and violence from bandits and renegade soldiers, with whom the country was swarming, God was personally right beside me— and He was just as personally right beside my congregation in the United States at the same time. I have been north off the shores of Labrador in Canada and south in Invercargill and Bluffs in New Zealand, the nearest to the South Pole of inhabited towns, and God was not only with me while I was there, but He is also there and everywhere all the time.

The book of Jeremiah tells us that God is always right *"at hand"* (Jer. 23:23) wherever we may be, but that He is at the same time *"afar off"* (v. 23) in the remotest spot not only in all the earth but in all the universe. He is even with those stars that are so far away that the light, traveling with the incredible and inconceivable rapidity with which light travels, takes six thousand years to get to us, so that the light you will see in the stars tonight will not be the light with which they shine tonight but the light that started to shine from them six thousand years ago. There is not one tiny spot in the whole universe where God is not. There is no spot in all the universe where a man can hide himself from God. He fills the heaven and He fills the earth; so *"says the LORD"* (Jer. 23:24), and the Lord always speaks the truth (Tit. 1:2).

Do you ask me how that can be? I confess that I do not know. Nor do I know how the air for five hundred miles around Los Angeles in every direction is filled with my voice and my words during my radio broadcasts, and at the same time is full of music and other voices as well, which are unheard until we turn on our radios and then tune to one radio station or another and hear them just as plainly as a man in the front row of my congregation can hear me when I am preaching. If my finite and feeble voice can be everywhere for five hundred miles around—perfectly hearable at any moment someone tunes in to his radio—is it hard to believe that an infinite God can be present at any and every moment everywhere in the universe that He Himself has created? It is not hard at all for me to believe it, but technology and its wonders have helped me to believe it. However, remember that the psalmist wrote about it twenty-nine hundred years before radio was dreamed of.

The most current legitimate science confirms the truth and inspiration of very ancient Scripture.

And yet men who call themselves scientists and philosophers deny the inspiration of those ancient *"holy men of God"* (2 Pet. 1:21) and imagine themselves to be the only real scientists and philosophers that there are in the whole world. Their minds have been confused by an extreme doctrine of "Devilution" that they term *evolution*. It would also be most fitting to change the first *o* in the word *evolution* into an *i* and call it "evilution."

WHAT DOES IT MEAN THAT GOD IS EVERYWHERE?

Before we go any further, let us consider some helpful, practical inferences from the great truth revealed in the Bible—a truth never dreamed of by man until the Bible revealed it—that God is everywhere.

God Can Be Worshipped Anywhere

First, God is not confined to temples or church buildings or buildings of any kind, but can be found and worshipped anywhere and everywhere beneath the shining sun by day or the glittering stars by night. The whole universe is a holy temple of God. We can enjoy His fellowship on some mountain peak, as I have done, or down in a mine one thousand feet beneath the earth and beneath the level of the sea, as I have also done. I believe in setting buildings apart for the service and worship of God, and I believe that it is the solemn duty of men and women to attend services there and to take their children there, if they can. In fact, I believe that men or women who do not go to the house set apart for the worship of God every Lord's Day, when they are able, and do not take all their children with them, if they can, are not good citizens. Nevertheless, I can meet God alone deep in the heart of the earth and upon the mountain peak, on Sunday and on other days, just as truly as I can meet Him in beautiful church buildings set apart by loving hands and grateful hearts for His worship and His glory.

God is everywhere, and the whole universe is His temple. That thought is not original with me, nor is it original with the modern poets. Paul declared it nearly two thousand years ago. Look again at what he said to that gathering of Stoic and Epicurean philosophers on the Areopagus in Athens in that ancient time. We find it in Acts 17:24–28:

> *God, who made the world and everything in it, since He is Lord of heaven and earth, does not dwell in temples made with hands. Nor is He worshiped with men's hands, as though He needed anything, since He gives to all life, breath, and all things. And He has made from one blood every nation of men to dwell on all the face of the earth, and has determined their preappointed times and the boundaries of their dwellings, so that they should seek the Lord, in the hope that they might grope for Him and find Him, though He is not far from each one of us; for in Him we live and move and have our being.*

Where did poor old Paul, whom some of our so-called very learned and very brilliant and still more self-sufficient modern theological professors and preachers are trying so hard to criticize and discredit, learn this? I will tell you where he learned it. He learned it directly from God through the Holy Spirit (2 Pet. 1:21). The person who, in the face of the clear facts of the case, doubts God's omnipresence is not in any proper usage of the word "rational"—as he dreams that he is and boasts that he is. He is utterly irrational—a determined, stubborn, willful blockhead. That is plain language, but it is also plain sense and undeniable fact.

Let us go back still further than Paul, more than seven hundred years before Paul, to Isaiah. Read this passage carefully:

> *For thus says the High and Lofty One who inhabits eternity, whose name is Holy: "**I dwell in the high and holy place, with him who has a contrite and humble spirit**, to revive the spirit of the humble, and to revive the heart of the contrite ones. For I will not contend forever, nor will I always be angry; for the spirit would fail before Me, and the souls which I have made. For the iniquity of his covetousness I was angry and struck him; I hid and was angry, and he went on backsliding in the way of his heart. I have seen his ways, and will heal him; I will also lead him, and restore comforts to him and to his mourners. I create the fruit of the lips: peace, peace **to him who is far off and to him who is near**," says the LORD, "and I will heal him." But the wicked are like the troubled sea, when it cannot rest, whose waters cast up mire and dirt. "There is no peace," says my God, "for the wicked."*
> *(Isa. 57:15–21, emphasis added)*

God Is Omnipresent

Where did old Isaiah learn this, living so long, long ago, twenty-five hundred years or more before our present-day theological seminaries were ever dreamed of? There is only one answer that even approaches reasonableness, and it is this: he was really inspired, undoubtedly inspired. He was inspired by God; his words were "God-breathed" (2 Tim. 3:16, literal Greek). And yet these learned gentlemen, these exponents of "the consensus of modern scholarship," blandly tell us that there is no such thing as supernatural inspiration and that Isaiah 57 was not written by Isaiah anyway! Well, then, by whom was it written? They answer, "Why,...by Mr. Deutero-Isaiah,* 'the Great Unknown.'"

No, it was not written by "the Great Unknown" but by one who was well-known to God, so well-known to God that God chose to speak through him. It was written by one who will still be well-known when these shallow and self-sufficient higher critics, Modernists, and New Theology men are forgotten forever. It was written by *"Isaiah the son of Amoz"* (Isa. 1:1), to whom God visibly appeared and whom He chose to be His mouthpiece, not only to the Jews of his own day but to all nations for all coming centuries. And his message is also for us today. (See Isaiah 6:1–8.)

God Can Deliver Anytime and Anywhere

The second inference from the great truth that God is everywhere is that God can always help and deliver those who trust Him. Since there is no place

---

* Meaning, "Mr. Secondary-Isaiah."

where God is not, there is no place where God cannot
come to the help and deliverance of His people. I may
live in the United States where the law is enforced, or
I may be in a continually war-ridden nation, or in the
heart of Africa—what difference does it make? God is
there as well as here.

Last summer, I watched a boat with armed men
in it who looked like bandits, of whom the sur-
rounding country was thought to be full, as it drew
near our unarmed boat, way up on the You River in
Hunan, China, just after sunset. It looked bad. Only
two or three days before, I had seen just such looking men fire upon and capture a Chinese *junk*, or
ship. It certainly did look scary, and one who knew
China far better than I whispered to me, "It looks
like a holdup." But my heart was quiet. God was
there, and I was silently talking to Him while I
watched the boat approach. Oh, I rejoice that I know
the God of the Bible and not the god of modern religious liberalism! I rejoice that my God is everywhere, and that He is not only everywhere but is
also, at the same time, a real God, a personal God,
an almighty and infinitely loving Father, and not the
mere cold, unreal, philosophical, impersonal, dead
"Absolute."

Nothing Can Be Hidden from God

The third inference from the great biblical truth
that God is everywhere is that you cannot hide anything you do or think or feel from God. The policy of
concealment governs the actions of all evildoers. We
witness it today in politics, in international affairs,
in the maladministration of justice, in business, in
the home, everywhere. The deputy sheriff takes a

bribe that he thinks no one sees and the prisoner does not go to San Quentin but escapes to the woods. The policeman takes a bribe on the sly, and the offender is not arrested. Murders are committed and clues that lead nowhere are paraded in the papers as being followed up, but clues that would lead to the guilty party are ignored. Nobody knows. Or does Someone know?

God is everywhere. He saw the murder and knows the guilty party, even if the officers of the law do not or do not want to. The adulterer goes on his damnable way under cover of night, and his wife and children do not know; they imagine that he is the best of fathers and the prince of husbands. Nobody knows. Or does Someone know? God knows. Yes, and He remembers, too, until just the right time comes, and then He will strike. Yes, God is everywhere; you cannot hide anything from Him. As the psalmist put it,

> *Where can I go from Your Spirit? Or where can I flee from Your presence? If I ascend into heaven, You are there; if I make my bed in hell [Sheol], behold, You are there. If I take the wings of the morning, and dwell in the uttermost parts of the sea, even there Your hand shall lead me, and Your right hand shall hold me. If I say, "Surely the darkness shall fall on me," even the night shall be light about me; indeed, the darkness shall not hide from You, but the night shines as the day; the darkness and the light are both alike to You.*
>
> *(Ps. 139:7–12)*

You have never committed a single sin that the holy God of the Bible, who is everywhere, does not know about. So you must pay the penalty for every sin of action or word or thought that you commit. You cannot escape. We may escape human avengers and human courts; we cannot escape God. Wearing the long white robes and hoods of the Ku Klux Klan, and using all sorts of foolish names of hobgoblins and whatnot when we go out to do our devilry, will not hide us from God. I am extremely glad of it. God is everywhere, unseen by all but seeing all. Therefore, apart from forgiveness and salvation in Christ Jesus, no sin, no matter how secret, will ever go unpunished—if not here, then in the next life. With a God who is present everywhere, every sin that man commits is a huge mistake.

God Is Not Only Near Us but He Will Also Protect Us

The fourth inference, and a glorious one it is, from the great truth of the Bible that God is everywhere is that it does not matter one particle if every earthly friend deserts us and every man on earth is against us, if we are true to God and conscience. God is not only near us but He will also protect us, and *"if God is for us, who can be against us?"* (Rom. 8:31).

Some thirty years ago, I incurred the deep enmity of some powerful and unscrupulous men. A man came to me with a warning. He named the men and spoke of their power and their unscrupulousness and how they had it in for me. I was not in the least disturbed. I knew that God is everywhere and that the plots and conspiracies of mere men would come to nothing. And I am still here.

IS GOD ANYWHERE IN PARTICULAR?

We have clearly seen that God is everywhere. Now another question arises: Is God anywhere in particular? Is God in certain places in a sense and in a fullness that He is not in other places? The Bible also answers these questions with unmistakable clearness.

Let us first look at John 14:28, which records the words of Jesus to His disciples. Let us pay close attention to His words:

> *You have heard Me say to you, "I am going away and coming back to you." If you loved Me, you would rejoice because I said, "I am going to the Father," for My Father is greater than I.*

Here our Lord distinctly said that, upon leaving His disciples and going into heaven, He was *"going to the Father."* So it is clear that God the Father is in heaven in a sense and in a fullness that He is not on earth.

Now let us look at the twentieth chapter of the same book:

> *Jesus said to* [Mary], *"Do not cling to Me, for I have not yet ascended to My Father; but go to My brethren and say to them, 'I am ascending to My Father and your Father, and to My God and your God.'"* (John 20:17)

In this verse, Jesus distinctly taught us that the Father is in heaven in a sense that He is not here on earth. In leaving the earth and ascending into heaven, He was ascending to God the Father, to a place where God the Father is in a sense that He is not here.

Next, let us read from the first chapter of Ephesians. Paul was speaking here about God and *"the exceeding greatness of His power toward us"* (v. 19). He wrote, *"Which He worked in Christ when He raised Him from the dead and seated Him at His right hand in the heavenly places"* (v. 20).

The meaning of these words is plain. They teach us that God has a specific habitation and that the Lord Jesus was exalted to a place at His right hand.

Let us now go to the book of Revelation:

> *Then I, John, saw the holy city, New Jerusalem, coming down out of heaven from God, prepared as a bride adorned for her husband.* [This clearly tells us that God is in heaven and that the New Jerusalem was coming down out of heaven from Him.] *And I heard a loud voice from heaven saying, "Behold, the tabernacle of God is with men, and He will dwell with them, and they shall be His people. God Himself will be with them and be their God."...And* [the angel] *carried me away in the Spirit to a great and high mountain, and showed me the great city, the holy Jerusalem, descending out of heaven from God....But I saw no temple in it, for the Lord God Almighty and the Lamb are its temple. The city had no need of the sun or of the moon to shine in it, for the glory of God illuminated it. The Lamb is its light.*
>
> (Rev. 21:2–3, 10, 22–23)

Next, let us look at Revelation 22:1, 3–4, where John continued,

> *And* [the angel] *showed me a pure river of water of life, clear as crystal, proceeding from the*

> *throne of God and of the Lamb....And there*
> *shall be no more curse, but the throne of God*
> *and of the Lamb shall be in it, and His ser-*
> *vants shall serve Him. They shall see His face,*
> *and His name shall be on their foreheads.*
>
> *(Rev. 22:1, 3–4)*

All these passages make it as clear as day that, while God is everywhere, as we have already seen, at the same time, it is also true that God is in one particular place, in heaven, in a way that He is not in any other place. We find this same truth in the Old Testament in Isaiah 66:1: *"Thus says the LORD: 'Heaven is My throne, and earth is My footstool. Where is the house that you will build Me? And where is the place of My rest?'"*

In this verse, heaven is said to be the *"throne"* of God, the place where He is especially and fully present, and the earth is said to be His *"footstool."* Clearly, then, there is a fullness and manifestation of God's presence in some place that there is not in other places. Heaven is the place where, at the present time, the presence and glory of God are especially and visibly manifested.

This great truth about God came out in a very striking and impressive way at the baptism of our Lord Jesus:

> *It came to pass in those days that Jesus came*
> *from Nazareth of Galilee, and was baptized by*
> *John in the Jordan. And immediately, coming*
> *up from the water, He saw the heavens parting*
> *and the Spirit descending upon Him like a*
> *dove. Then a voice came from heaven, "You*

> *are My beloved Son, in whom I am well*
> *pleased."*   *(Mark 1:9–11)*

In this passage, we are distinctly told that the voice of God speaking to His beloved Son *"came from heaven."* In the marvelous prayer that our Lord taught us, He instructed us to address God as *"our Father in heaven* [more literally, "in the heavens"]" (Matt. 6:9). It is clear, then, that although God is everywhere, He must be "in the heavens" in a sense that He is not here on earth.

God the Father is especially manifested in heaven at the present time. God the Son, during the days of our Lord's life and ministry here on earth, was especially manifested on earth. However, note that He Himself told us in John 3:13 that even while He was on earth, He was in heaven. His words are, *"No one has ascended to heaven but He who came down from heaven, that is, the Son of Man **who is in heaven"*** (emphasis added). God the Son is now in heaven, having ascended there from the Mount of Olives forty days after His resurrection from the dead. (See Acts 1:1–11; 7:55–56; Ephesians 1:19–20; and many other passages.) God the Holy Spirit is manifested everywhere: in creation (see Genesis 1:2; Psalm 104:30); in all believers (see John 14:16–17; Romans 8:9); and with unbelievers (see John 16:7–11).

Through the Spirit, the Father and the Son dwell today in the believer in Jesus Christ (see John 14:17–20, 23); They dwell personally in him. Our Lord Jesus is with us (if we go out to do His work) until the end of this present dispensation. Jesus said in Matthew 28:18–20,

God Is Omnipresent

All authority has been given to Me in heaven and on earth. Go therefore and make disciples of all the nations, baptizing them in the name of the Father and of the Son and of the Holy Spirit, teaching them to observe all things that I have commanded you; and lo, I am with you always, even to the end of the age.

But God the Father is especially and personally present in heaven today in a sense that He is not with us here. God the Son, in a glorified human form, is presently in heaven, waiting until that glad Day when He will come back to this earth to receive us and take us up with Him into glory.

I meet God face-to-face now. Though I do not see Him, nevertheless, I have real, intimate, personal communion with Him now. But when my earthly pilgrimage and warfare are over, I will meet Him and *see* Him in heaven in a sense and in a fullness that I do not meet Him and see Him now. And then, in that wonderful day, as David put it so many centuries ago, *"I shall be satisfied, when I awake, with beholding thy form"* (Ps. 17:15 ASV).

Chapter 5

God Is the Eternal I Am

God said to Moses, "I AM WHO I AM."
—Exodus 3:14

In the last chapter, we saw that God is everywhere but that He manifests Himself in the fullness of His presence and glory in heaven in a way that He does not manifest Himself here on earth. In this chapter, we will come to understand that God is the Eternal I AM. He always was, always is, and always will be. And He is always the same.

Let us begin by looking at several Scripture passages that illustrate this truth:

Then Abraham planted a tamarisk tree in Beersheba, and there called on the name of the LORD [Jehovah], the Everlasting God.
                    (Gen. 21:33)

Then Moses said to God, "Indeed, when I come to the children of Israel and say to them, 'The God of your fathers has sent me to you,' and they say to me, 'What is His name?' what shall I say to them?" And God said to Moses,

WHO I AM." And He said, "Thus you shall say to the children of Israel, 'I AM has sent me to you.'" Moreover God said to Moses, "Thus you shall say to the children of Israel: 'The LORD God of your fathers, the God of Abraham, the God of Isaac, and the God of Jacob, has sent me to you. This is My name forever, and this is My memorial to all generations.'"

(Exod. 3:13–15)

Have you not known? Have you not heard? The everlasting God, the LORD [Jehovah], the Creator of the ends of the earth, neither faints nor is weary. His understanding is unsearchable. (Isa. 40:28)

LORD, You have been our dwelling place in all generations. Before the mountains were brought forth, or ever You had formed the earth and the world, even from everlasting to everlasting, You are God. You turn man to destruction, and say, "Return, O children of men." For a thousand years in Your sight are like yesterday when it is past, and like a watch in the night. (Ps. 90:1–4)

I said, "O my God, do not take me away in the midst of my days; Your years are throughout all generations. Of old You laid the foundation of the earth, and the heavens are the work of Your hands. They will perish, but You will endure; yes, they will all grow old like a garment; like a cloak You will change them, and they will be changed. But You are the same, and Your years will have no end."

(Ps. 102:24–27)

All these passages of Scripture are from the Old Testament, and two of the five are from the first two books of the Bible. These passages were written thousands of years ago, and Abraham called on *"the Everlasting God"* approximately thirty-eight hundred years ago. Yet these passages present to us a conception of God of the profoundest philosophical wisdom and of the highest conceivable sublimity, unequaled by anything even in this day of advanced thinking, except insofar as men have derived their thoughts of God from the Bible.

How did Abraham, Moses, Isaiah, and David, living in such a faraway past, many centuries before even the earliest heathen philosophers had worked out their vague and indefinite and now entirely antiquated conceptions of God, arrive at such a high view of God? There is only one rational answer to such a question, namely, that God Himself supernaturally revealed Himself to them and declared to them these great truths about Himself.

The Bible is, beyond an honest question, even in its most ancient parts, a supernatural Book, a supernatural revelation; the unique and inerrant inspiration of the Bible is a scientifically proven fact. Modern religious liberals and biblical critics have made laborious, scholarly, subtle, and determined efforts to prove the contrary and to make us believe that a supernatural revelation and inerrant inspiration are impossibilities. But the actual facts in the case, evidenced by the Scriptures, demonstrate the utter foolishness of their so-called science. They are not scientists; they demonstrate only superficial knowledge.

The God of the Bible

God Always Is

The first thing that these sublime utterances of Abraham, Moses, Isaiah, and David make clear is that God is the Eternal I Am. With Him there is neither past nor future; it is all one eternal present. God never began to be, and He will never cease to be. God always is.

Our present-day scientists are telling us of the vast antiquity of the globe on which we live, which we call Earth. They once talked of the many thousands of years that it had been in existence, but now they talk of the many millions and billions of years of its existence. That is very largely guesswork, and guesswork of the most baseless character; but they have so constantly reiterated their guesses that their theories now have all the force of scientifically proven certainty. With the average scientist of the present day, the constant repetition of a hypothesis, of a wild guess, or even of a lie, has all the force of scientific demonstration. Ask him how he knows that the evolutionary hypothesis, even in its most sweeping and daring and utterly unsubstantiated forms, is true, and he replies, "Why, all scientists are agreed about it." Yes, but why are they agreed about it? Upon what scientifically ascertained facts and inescapably logical inferences from those facts do they base their opinion? If you ask him these questions, again, all you get is the reply that "they are all agreed about it."

This form of argument has no weight whatsoever with anyone who is familiar with the history of scientific and philosophical opinions and who therefore knows that, over and over again, through the many centuries of human thinking, all the philosophers and all the scientists have been perfectly agreed upon what we now know to be error. If anyone is well-informed and is also fair-minded, he will not accept any theory simply on the ground of a statement that "all scientists are agreed about it."

When you ask this type of scientist how he knows that there was not only a caveman or cavemen, as of course we all know there have been and still are, but how he knows that the whole present human race descended from primitive cavemen, again he replies, "All scientists are agreed about it." But why are they agreed about it? Is there any scientific or historical proof that the races living upon Earth today are descended from a primitive caveman, a man part beast and part man? He replies, again, "All scientists are agreed about it." Yes, but *why* are they agreed about it? Every particle of real evidence about the men of thousands of years ago is that they were men of a high type intellectually and that they had worked out a fine and well-developed civilization.

But suppose the scientists are right in this matter of the vast antiquity of the Earth; suppose that this Earth *is* millions or billions of years old. Nothing in the first chapter of Genesis, properly understood and literally interpreted, proves that it is not; for the careful and thorough student of the first chapter of Genesis knows that there is a great gap of no one knows how many centuries or millennia between Genesis 1:1 and Genesis 1:3. So, even if these suppositions that this Earth is hundreds of millions or billions of years old are true—even in that case—when this Earth began to exist, when the stars and sun and moon began to be, *God already existed.*

In the very first verse in the Bible, God is seen *"in the beginning"* as already existing and as "[creating] *the heavens and the earth.*" Go back, back, back, back, endlessly and eternally back, and God always is. Speaking to Moses out in the desert over thirty-four hundred years ago, when Moses asked who He was, Jehovah replied, *"I AM WHO I AM"* (Exod. 3:14). He said, "My name is I AM. I am the Eternal I AM." (See verse 14.)

There is an eternity behind us as well as an eternity ahead of us. The God of the Bible is, as Isaiah said in one place, *"the High and Lofty One who inhabits eternity"* (Isa. 57:15). Eternity has no end at either end, ahead of us or behind us, and God is through it all. God has no beginning and no ending.

Of course, it is impossible for the finite mind to conceive of eternity, especially of an eternity behind us. When we try to think of an eternity behind us, the question inevitably arises with every really thoughtful person: if there is an endless eternity behind us, then how did we ever get to the present moment? And, of course, we cannot answer it. But the idea that there is *not* an eternity behind us is equally inconceivable to the finite mind. For if you say that there is not an eternity behind us, the question inevitably arises: if there is not an eternity behind us, go back to the starting point, however many millions or billions of years behind us that may be; what was before that? Again, no answer is possible, and you have landed in an equally unfathomable and impenetrable fog of impossibility and inconceivability.

There is an eternity behind us; there must be. The utterly inconceivable is, at the same time, the

certainly true. God, throughout all the eternity behind us, is the Eternal I AM. He is the Eternal I AM
today. And in the eternity still ahead of us, He will
always be the Eternal I AM. As the psalmist put it
(and, by the way, in this instance Moses himself was
the psalmist), *"Even from everlasting to everlasting,
You are God"* (Ps. 90:2).

In the last chapter, we saw how the New Testament critics and Modernists are trying to discredit
the apostle Paul, and thereby are in reality discrediting themselves. The Old Testament critics have
turned their heaviest artillery upon Moses in order
to discredit him even if they cannot discredit anyone
else. We see from the Scripture passages that we
have just looked at that, by so doing, they also are
discrediting themselves. The God of Moses, who
wrote about 1450 B.C., is a far greater and far more
wonderful Being than the god of any of the Modern-
ist professors of theology today.

The very name *Jehovah*—the distinctive name
of the God of Abraham, Isaac, and Jacob; the God of
the Old Testament; and the God of our Lord and
Savior Jesus Christ—also sets forth this great truth
of the eternity of God. The name *Jehovah* is derived
from the frequently used Hebrew verb meaning "to
be" (in the first person, present, indicative, "I am").
It presents the thought that God is eternal and im-
mutable (unchangeable), the Eternally Existing One,
One "who will never be other than He is." The significance of the name *Jehovah* comes out clearly in
two of the texts that we looked at earlier: Genesis
21:33 and Isaiah 40:28. You will see this if you study
these texts carefully, which we do not have time to
do now.

No words of human comment can add anything to the sublimity of this divinely given biblical conception of God. The wonderful truth of the eternity of God, that God is the Eternal I AM, is not one so much to be commented upon as to be meditated upon by each one of us, alone, in *"the secret place"* (Ps. 91:1), until our souls are filled with wonder, awe, adoration, worship, and unhesitating and absolute faith.

In view of this great truth about God, we see new significance in the words our Lord Jesus spoke in His prayer on the night before His crucifixion: *"And this is eternal life, that they may know You, the only true God, and Jesus Christ whom You have sent"* (John 17:3). We also see new significance in John's words in his first epistle, written undoubtedly not only by inspiration but also with the words of our Lord in mind:

> *We know that the Son of God has come and has given us an understanding, that we may know Him who is true; and we are in Him who is true, in His Son Jesus Christ. This is the true God and eternal life. Little children, keep yourselves from idols.* (1 John 5:20–21)

In the revelation of God in the Bible, we find this attribute of eternity ascribed not only to the Father but also to the Son, Jesus Christ. In the second chapter of Philippians, we are told of the Divine Person who emptied Himself of His divine form and divine glory and took upon Himself *"the form of a servant, and was made in the likeness of men"* (v. 7 KJV). He thus became incarnate in the person of Jesus of Nazareth and *"became obedient unto death, even the death of the cross"* (v. 8 KJV). This Divine Person, before becoming incarnate, *"exist*[ed] *in the form of God"* (v. 6 ASV). The Greek participle in verse six translated *"existing"* in the American Standard Edition of the Revised Version and *"being"* in the King James Version is a distinctive and deeply significant word. It seems to indicate "to exist originally" or "being originally" (RV, margin). In any case, the verse points to the eternal preexistence of our Lord Jesus Christ. The same thought is found in John 1:1, where we are told that the Eternal Word who became flesh (v. 14) in the person of Jesus of Nazareth already *"was"* *"in the beginning."* The exact words are: *"In the beginning was the Word"* (John 1:1). That is, in the very beginning of all created things, He already was. We find the same thought again in Hebrews 1:6–12, where in speaking of Jesus Christ, the Son of God, the writer said,

> *But when* [God] *again brings the firstborn into the world, He says: "Let all the angels of God worship Him." And of the angels He says: "Who makes His angels spirits and His ministers a flame of fire." But to the Son He says: "Your throne, O God, is forever and ever; a scepter of righteousness is the scepter of Your Kingdom. You have loved righteousness and hated lawlessness; therefore God, Your God, has anointed You with the oil of gladness more than Your companions." And: "You, LORD, in the beginning laid the foundation of the earth, and the heavens are the work of Your hands.*

*They will perish, but You remain; and they
will all grow old like a garment; like a cloak
You will fold them up, and they will be
changed. But You are the same, and Your
years will not fail."* (Heb. 1:6–12)

The eternity of the third Person of the Divine
Trinity, the Holy Spirit, is also taught in the Bible.
For example, in Hebrews 9:14, He is spoken of as
"The eternal Spirit." Father, Son, and Holy Spirit
are the one Jehovah, the Eternal I AM. They existed
from all eternity and will exist to all eternity.

In this wondrous truth of the eternity of the triune God of the Bible, we get the answer to the question that very shallow and very foolish agnostics or
atheists ask when we earnestly claim that the signs
of intelligent design everywhere in the universe,
from the largest star to the minutest microscopic
organisms, prove the existence of an intelligent De-
signer and Creator: "Then who made God?" The
great truth we are now studying answers this question. He was never made; He never began to be. He
always was, He always is, and He always will be.

GOD IS ALWAYS THE SAME

Yet the Bible teaches us not only that God is the
Eternal I AM, that He always *is*, from all eternity
and to all eternity, but also that He is always the
same. In James 1:17, we read: *"Every good gift and
every perfect gift is from above, and comes down from
the Father of lights, with whom there is no variation
or shadow of turning."* The metaphor used in this
verse refers to the changing phases of the moon and

some of the other heavenly bodies. The thought is that there are no variations with God as there are with the moon, but that He is ever and always the same. We find the same great truth in the Old Testament. In Malachi 3:6, Jehovah declares, *"I am the LORD, I do not change."*

God never changes in His character or His purposes. He is ever always just the same, from all eternity and to all eternity. The extreme evolutionists tell us that there is a constant evolution or change going on in all forms of being. This is not true. In the one and only Being who has existed from all eternity, there has not been one particle of change from all eternity behind us, and there will be none to all eternity ahead of us. Someone may ask, "If this is true, how is it, then, that we are told in Jonah 3:10, *'Then God saw* [the Ninevites'] *works, that they turned from their evil way; and God relented from the disaster that He had said He would bring upon them, and He did not do it'*?" The answer to this seemingly puzzling question is very simple. It is precisely because God did not change, precisely because He remained absolutely the same in His character—infinitely hating sin—and in His purpose to punish sin with judgment, that when Nineveh changed in its attitude toward sin, God necessarily changed in His attitude toward Nineveh and in His dealings with Nineveh.

Again, this is precisely because He did not change in His character. If God always remains the same, if His attitude toward sin and righteousness is unchanging, then His dealings with men must change as they turn from sin to repentance. His character remains forever the same, and His purpose in regard to how to deal with sin always remains the same. But for that very reason, His dealings with men change as they change from a position that is hateful to His unchangeable hatred of sin to one that is pleasing to His unchangeable love of righteousness.

But the objector will still ask, "If it is true that God is always the same, how then is it that we are told in Genesis 6:6–7, *'And it repented Jehovah that he had made man on the earth, and it grieved him at his heart. And Jehovah said, I will destroy man whom I have created'* (ASV)?" This question may seem a little more puzzling than the former one, but the answer to this one is also simple: Man's wickedness had become so great on this earth and so abhorrent to God that His very creation, which God Himself had brought to pass, was the object of great grief to Him. This was not because God had changed but because He remained the same as He always had been in His infinite hatred of sin. This does not necessarily imply that God wished, all things considered, that He had not created man. It only means just exactly what it says, that because of man's great and ever increasing sin, it *"grieved"* God *"that he had made man on the earth."*

Many things that you and I do are a grief to us, and yet, everything considered, we do not wish that we had not done them. When the Bible says that *"it repented Jehovah that he had made man,"* it means, as the context clearly shows, that He turned from His creative dealings with man to His destroying dealings. As the Bible puts it, *"And Jehovah said, I will destroy man whom I have created from the face of the ground"* (Gen. 6:7 ASV). This destruction of man whom He had created was necessitated by man's sin; the unchangeably holy God had to destroy man who had become so sunken in sin.

We live in an ever changing world. The world has changed more rapidly in the twentieth century in its business, politics, and international relations; in its civilization and dominant ideas; in its science and philosophy; and in its ethics and religion than in any other period of its history. Amid the startling and sometimes appalling changes that are taking place in men and women, sometimes in the men and women we know most intimately and love most dearly, what a comfort and joy it is to know that there is one Being who never changes one particle, that He is always the same—*"the same yesterday, today, and forever"* (Heb. 13:8). When your head is bewildered and your heart is sick amid the rapid changes that are taking place to-day in institutions, in things, and in men, and even in preachers and other religious leaders, just look up to God and behold Him and rejoice in Him as the One who is always absolutely the same—the same in His infinite wisdom, the same in His infinite righteous-ness, the same in His infinite holiness, the same in His infinite power, and the same in His infinite love. There is scarcely another thought in the whole scope of the glorious truth of the Bible more comforting than that. Oh, I not only worship and adore but also rejoice in and rest in this God of the Bible, the un-changeable God, God the Father, Son, and Holy Spirit.

GOD IS SELF-EXISTENT

There is another thought that we must consider in connection with the eternity and immutability of

God, the God of the Bible, *"the only true God"* (John 17:3). Not only has God always existed and always been the same, but God is also self-existent. God not only exists from all eternity, but He also exists *from Himself.* This tremendous thought is found in our Lord's own words in John 5:26, where He said, *"The Father has life in Himself."* He does not have life derived from anyone else or from anything else, but He has *"life in Himself."* He is self-existent. Our Lord added, regarding Himself, the second Person of the Divine Trinity, that the Father had given to Him also to have life in Himself: *"As the Father has life in Himself, so He has granted the Son to have life in Himself"* (v. 26).

The same great thought is also found in the most profound philosophical discourse that was ever delivered on this earth, Paul's sermon on the Areopagus in Athens to the Epicurean and Stoic philosophers, recorded in Acts 17:24–28:

> *God, who made the world and everything in it, since He is Lord of heaven and earth, does not dwell in temples made with hands. Nor is He worshiped with men's hands, as though He needed anything, since He gives to all life, breath, and all things. And He has made from one blood every nation of men to dwell on all the face of the earth, and has determined their preappointed times and the boundaries of their dwellings, so that they should seek the Lord, in the hope that they might grope for Him and find Him, though He is not far from each one of us; for in Him we live and move and have our being.*

In this thought, that God is eternally self-existent, we again have the answer to the very foolish atheistic question mentioned earlier, "Who made God?" The self-evident answer is, "He was not made; He is eternally self-existent."

Such is the God of the Bible, the only God whom the true Christian worships, the God whom to know is eternal life, *the only true God"* (John 17:3). Well might John—who himself recorded so many of these statements of Jesus Christ and who also wrote so many profound statements about God—well might he say in 1 John 5:20–21,

> *We know that the Son of God has come and has given us an understanding, that we may know Him who is true; and we are in Him who is true, in His Son Jesus Christ. This is the true God and eternal life. Little children, keep yourselves from idols* [in other words, from any god but this God].

GOD IS WORTHY OF ALL OUR TRUST

Just one more thought in closing: Since God always was and always will be, and since He is always the same, who is as worthy of our unwavering confidence and our absolute surrender as He is? And what is so worthy of our unhesitating confidence as His Word? The history of human science and human philosophy since the dawn of man's thinking and reasoning has been a history of constant change. What all philosophers and scientists regard today as forever settled is entirely unsettled tomorrow. What all scientists accept in one century, such as, for example, the

Ptolemaic system (or theory of the universe), is rejected by all scientists of another century. The well-established science of today is the butt of the ridicule of all the thinking men of tomorrow. But God's thought never changes; it is always the same, and it is always true. What fools we are, then, to give up the unchanging and eternally true Word of the self-existent, eternal, and eternally unchanging God for the ever changing scientific and philosophical theories of constantly changing man.

Chapter 6

GOD IS OMNIPOTENT

Is anything too hard for the LORD?
—Genesis 18:14

In the last chapter, we saw that God is the Eternal I AM. He always was, He always is, and He always will be. He is always the same, and He is self-existent.

The topic of this chapter is: God is omnipotent. God can do all things; there is nothing too hard for Him. I have chosen six Scripture verses that illustrate this theme:

[Job said,] *"I know that You can do everything, and that no purpose of Yours can be withheld from You."*   (Job 42:2)

Is anything too hard for the Lord?
                                (Gen. 18:14)

In the beginning God created the heavens and the earth.   (Gen. 1:1)

[Jeremiah prayed,] *"Ah, Lord GOD! Behold, You have made the heavens and the earth by*

Your great power and outstretched arm. There is nothing too hard for You."...Then the word of the LORD came to Jeremiah, saying, "Behold, I am the LORD, the God of all flesh. Is there anything too hard for Me?"

(Jer. 32:17, 26–27)

Then God said, "Let there be light"; and there was light.   *(Gen. 1:3)*

Jesus looked at them and said to them, "With men this is impossible, but with God all things are possible."   *(Matt. 19:26)*

You will note that five of these six texts are from the Old Testament. Three of them are from the first book in the Bible, and one is from the book of Job, which is regarded by many scholars as one of the oldest books of the Bible and by some as the very oldest book. One of these texts is the very first verse in the Bible, and one of the most remarkable and significant of the texts is the third verse in the Bible. Some of these passages, so elevated both in their thought and in their expression of the thought, were written about thirty-four hundred years ago, and there is every reason to suppose that Moses derived his account of Creation from much earlier sources. So I again ask the question that I asked in a previous chapter: How did Job, Jeremiah, and Moses, living in such a faraway past, many centuries before even the earliest heathen philosophers had worked out their vague, indefinite, inadequate, and now entirely antiquated conceptions of God, arrive at such a high view of God? In reply, I declare again that there is only one answer to such a question that has in it even the remotest approach to reasonableness. It is this: God supernaturally revealed Himself to those men and declared to them these exalted truths about Himself. The Bible is, beyond question, even in its earliest and most ancient parts, a supernatural Book, a supernatural revelation; the unique and inerrant inspiration of the Bible in all its parts is a scientifically proven fact.

The doctrine that the Bible presents to us a revelation given directly by God to men whom He Himself had chosen for that purpose, and who spoke and wrote as they were inspired (2 Tim. 3:16) and were "borne along" in their utterances by the Holy Spirit (see 2 Peter 1:21), is scientifically demonstrated. It is an inescapable conclusion from facts that are right before us. The doctrine of the divine inspiration of the Bible is demanded and necessitated by the inexorable logic of facts, not merely facts from long, long ago but present-day facts that we can see for ourselves with our own eyes.

Among the many fantastic theories of higher criticism is the much cherished one that the account of Creation in the Bible was derived from the early Accadian (Babylonian) traditions. But the Accadian accounts contain no exalted teachings about God such as we find in the Bible. On the contrary, their infantile mythology is replete with the most childish and now utterly discarded fancies about the birth of the gods. The Bible's representations of God stand apart not only from all the literature or fragments of literature of that day but from the literature of all days. They stand apart even from the literature of our own day—a day of supposedly singular enlightenment—except insofar as the literature of today has borrowed its views of God from this old, old Book.

GOD CAN DO ANYTHING

The first thing that these exalted, matchless, and obviously divinely inspired utterances of Job, Jeremiah, Moses, and our Lord Jesus Himself make clear is that there is no limit whatsoever to the power of the God of the Bible; there is nothing He cannot do. There is nothing, absolutely nothing, too hard for Him.

What a heartening, delightful, and overwhelmingly thrilling, as well as awe-inspiring, thought it is that there is one Being in this universe whose power has no limits. He can do absolutely anything He wills to do; He can do it by His mere will and word, and do it in the instant He wills it, not by a slow, age-requiring process of evolution. All the comfort, all the joy, and all the soul-stirring inspiration there is in that thought can only be felt when we put it in conjunction with the moral character of the Being who possesses this power—His righteousness, His holiness, His love, and His mercy—and in conjunction with the relationship of this omnipotent God to us—namely, that He is our Father, the Father of everyone who truly believes in His Son Jesus Christ.

But let us now go somewhat into detail, as the Bible itself does, in presenting this truth of the omnipotence of God, a truth that is so wonderful and so glorious.

ALL OF CREATION IS SUBJECT TO GOD

In the first place, all of creation is subject to the will and Word of God. This means not only the whole earth, but also all the innumerable stars, billions of them, each one of them of such vast magnitude that our minds cannot take it in, and in comparison with which our whole planet is but a mere speck. All these inconceivably vast worlds are subject to the will and Word of God. Look at what David said in Psalm 33:6–9:

> By the word of the LORD the heavens were made, and all the host of them by the breath of His mouth. He gathers the waters of the sea together as a heap; He lays up the deep in storehouses. Let all the earth fear the LORD; let all the inhabitants of the world stand in awe of Him. For He spoke, and it was done; He commanded, and it stood fast.

Read also what Jehovah, the Everlasting God, the Eternal I AM, said through Nahum, one of the older prophets, predating Ezekiel and Jeremiah:

> The LORD is slow to anger and great in power, and will not at all acquit the wicked. The LORD has His way in the whirlwind and in the storm, and the clouds are the dust of His feet. He rebukes the sea and makes it dry, and dries up all the rivers. Bashan and Carmel wither, and the flower of Lebanon wilts. The mountains quake before Him, the hills melt, and the earth heaves at His presence, yes, the world and all who dwell in it. Who can stand before His indignation? And who can endure the fierceness of His anger? His fury is poured out like fire, and the rocks are thrown down by Him. (Nah. 1:3–6)

Merely as literature, what can match in vividness, force, splendor, and sublimity of expression these utterances of this man of long, long ago, whom God inspired (2 Tim. 3:16) and whose writings Paul declared were "God-breathed" (v. 16, literal Greek)? We can see for ourselves today that this statement of Paul's must be true.

But I have reserved one brief statement that rises to loftier heights than all of these:

> *In the beginning God created the heavens and the earth. The earth was without form, and void; and darkness was on the face of the deep. And the Spirit of God was hovering over* ["was brooding upon," ASV, margin] *the face of the waters. Then God said, "Let there be light"; and there was light.*　　(Gen. 1:1-3)

Notice especially the closing words, *"Then God said, 'Let there be light'; and there was light."* That is one of the most remarkable sentences that was ever written—remarkable in its sublimity and remarkable also in its beauty, brevity, and simplicity. The Hebrew text, literally translated, is even more remarkable. Let me give you an exact, literal translation: "And God said, Light be; and Light was."

Our sons and daughters are being taught in our colleges, and even our little boys and girls in our public schools, and sometimes even in some of our Sunday schools, that the first chapter of Genesis is only folklore. Let me say, in light of the facts, that to say that the first chapter of Genesis is folklore is foolishness, no matter how learned and scientific the gentlemen may claim to be who indulge in this kind of thoroughly infantile nonsense. Genesis 1:1–3, written so many centuries before modern science and philosophy were dreamed of, bears the unmistakable marks of divine inspiration. The very first verses of the Bible bear the unmistakable stamp and seal of their divine origin.

ALL OF MANKIND IS SUBJECT TO GOD

In the second place, not only is all of creation subject to God's will and Word, but all of mankind is also subject to the will and Word of God. Read James 4:13–15:

> Come now, you who say, "Today or tomorrow we will go to such and such a city, spend a year there, buy and sell, and make a profit"; whereas you do not know what will happen tomorrow. For what is your life? It is even a vapor that appears for a little time and then vanishes away. Instead you ought to say, "If the Lord wills, we shall live and do this or that."

What God wills, man must do. There is no thwarting the purpose of God, and there is no subverting His Word. What God promises and what God threatens are both as absolutely sure to be done as if they were already accomplished. We form our plans and marshal our resources, and sometimes they seem very great; indeed, they seem invincible and irresistible. But if God plans otherwise, all our wisest schemes and all our most determined and most powerful efforts come to nothing. We say, "I will do this or that," and it seems as if nothing could prevent us; but how often man's impotent "I will" is met by God's omnipotent "I won't." This is what we would more wisely say: *"If the Lord wills, we shall live and do this or that"* (James 4:15). If the Lord *won't*, then we won't do this or that, no matter how irresistible the forces that are at our command may seem. We have it constantly proclaimed in our ears in this day of man's magnificent self-confidence that "the will is omnipotent." Yes, the will is omnipotent, but *whose* will? God's will, Jehovah's will—and His alone. All of creation and all of mankind must do His will.

Happy is the person who voluntarily and gladly subjects himself to God's will and Word. We would far better do it from choice; for in the ultimate outcome, we will have to do it anyway. And there is all the difference between heaven and hell in doing the will of God voluntarily or doing it by compulsion. *For do it we must.*

Napoleon was the ablest general of his day, and probably of all time. At the same time, he was the most adroit politician the world has ever seen, and he was also a man of the most unconquerable will. He willed to have the whole world at his feet, and it seemed as if it would be, as if nothing could prevent it. But God willed otherwise. When Napoleon tried to invade Russia, God spoke, and the soft and gentle snowflakes fell and fell and fell, and kept on falling, and Napoleon Bonaparte fell also. His army was decimated and his reign shortly came to an end.

Kaiser Wilhelm also determined to rule the world with "Deutschland über alles," or "Germany above everything else." Years went into the preparation, marvelously ingenious preparation, of the best-trained armed forces the world ever knew—the best guns, the mightiest navy, unconquerable and almost innumerable submarines, wonderful fortresses, mighty Zeppelin airships that filled London with terror and came within an inch of laying it in ruins, destructive gases the world had never dreamed of, and much more. It seemed as if Germany would inevitably conquer. But Kaiser Wilhelm's "I will" was met by the Lord God Almighty's "I won't." The army was scattered, the navy and submarines were scrapped, the Zeppelins became ashes, the gases evaporated, and Helgoland Island was dynamited and dismantled—a pile of expensive rubbish.

The whole human race and every member of it, from emperor to blind beggar or outcast leper, is subject to the will and Word of God. The time is fast approaching when all who have sought to withstand His will,

> the kings of the earth, the great men, the rich men, the commanders, the mighty men, every slave and every free man, [will hide] themselves in the caves and in the rocks of the mountains, and [will say] to the mountains and rocks, "Fall on us and hide us from the face of Him who sits on the throne and from the wrath of the Lamb! For the great day of His wrath has come, and who is able to stand?" (Rev. 6:15–17)

Yes, the time is fast approaching when not only will the will of God be irresistible (as it is today), but the whole world will also know it and all will hear,

> as it were, the voice of a great multitude, as the sound of many waters and as the sound of

117

mighty thunderings, saying, "Alleluia! For the
Lord God Omnipotent reigns!"   (Rev. 19:6)

I am not greatly troubled about the scheming
and plans of conquest of other nations, about the
plots and co-conspiracies of other countries, even if
they do have huge populations. I am not troubled
about the failure of well-intentioned political trea-
ties. In spite of all these things and everything else, I
know that God is omnipotent, that He reigns (Rev.
19:6), that "[His] *kingdom* [will] *come* [and His] *will*
[will] *be done on earth as it is in heaven*" (Matt.
6:10), and that, in due time, *"the kingdoms of this*
world [will] *become the kingdoms of our Lord and of*
His Christ, and He shall reign forever and ever!"
(Rev. 11:15).

Anyone who truly and intelligently believes in
the God of the Bible is bound to be an optimist. I am
sometimes asked, "How can you be such a constant
optimist under present conditions?" I will tell you: it
is because I believe in God, the God of the Bible. Oh,
it is a great thing to really believe in the God of the
Bible, an omnipotent God, a God for whom absolutely *nothing* is too hard, who can do *anything*. I
would rather believe in such a God and not have a
penny in my pocket at the present moment than not
believe in Him and have a billion dollars in the bank
awaiting my call. Oh, you who have your thousands
and millions of dollars, keep them! Give me God.

ANGELS ARE SUBJECT TO GOD

Third, all the angels are subject to the will and
Word of God. In Hebrews 1:13–14, we read:

To which of the angels has He ever said: "Sit at My right hand, till I make Your enemies Your footstool"? Are they not all ministering spirits sent forth to minister for those who will inherit salvation?

We constantly think of men, the intelligent beings who in a bodily and visible form inhabit this globe, as being the only intelligences in the universe. How absurd! It is absurd not only from the standpoint of the teaching of the Bible but also from the standpoint of a carefully observant science and of common sense. Imagine thinking that we are the only intelligences in this vast world, to whose stupendous magnitude science is beginning to open our eyes! It is ridiculous! No, there are countless angelic hosts with different ranks among them—*"principalities," "powers," "world rulers," "spiritual hosts,"* "authorities," and "dominions." (See Ephesians 1:21; 6:12.) These angelic hosts have wisdom and power far transcending that of men. All the vast, innumerable, powerful angelic hosts are at God's command; every one of them is subject to His will and His Word. Therefore, I cannot see why I should not sing in the midst of any seeming dangers, when confronted and surrounded by countless enemies, as David sang of old,

The LORD is my light and my salvation; whom shall I fear? The LORD is the strength of my life; of whom shall I be afraid? When the wicked came against me to eat up my flesh, my enemies and foes, they stumbled and fell. Though an army may encamp against me, my

*heart shall not fear; though war should rise
against me, in this I will be confident.*

(Ps. 27:1–3)

THE DEVIL IS SUBJECT TO GOD

Fourth, the Devil is absolutely subject to the will
and Word of our omnipotent God. This comes out
very plainly in the first and second chapters of the
book of Job. I suggest that you read these two chapters through entirely. In the first chapter, we are
told how Satan maligned Job before God and asked
for the privilege of striking down everything Job
owned, saying that if God would permit him to take
Job's property away, Job would renounce Jehovah to
His face. Jehovah agreed to allow Satan to destroy
all that belonged to Job, but He did not permit Satan
to touch Job's body. So we see that Satan could do
only what Jehovah permitted him to do. He could
not go one step further than God said he could.

In the second chapter, Satan appears again and
maligns Job and tells Jehovah that if He will permit
him to touch Job's *"bone and his flesh"* (Job 2:5),
that Job will renounce Jehovah to His face. This
time Satan is permitted to touch Job's body but is
compelled to *"spare his life"* (v. 6). Again we see that
Satan, even with all his power, could go no further,
not one inch further, than Jehovah permitted him to
go. So we see that Satan himself is subject to the will
and Word of God, and can only do what God, for His
own wise purposes, permits. As great as the Devil is
in cunning and in power, a person who is in fellowship with the omnipotent God has no need to fear
him.

God Is Omnipotent

To sum up all that we have seen so far, all of creation is absolutely subject to God's will and Word; all of mankind is absolutely subject to God's will and Word; all the angels, fallen and unfallen, are subject to God's will and Word; and Satan himself is absolutely subject to God's will and Word. God is omnipotent. He can do anything; He can do all things. There is nothing, absolutely nothing, too hard for Him. There are countless blessed and glorious applications of and inferences from this great truth, but we do not have time now to consider them. You must make these applications and inferences for yourself; however, it will take you your whole lifetime to discover them all, and you will rejoice in them throughout all eternity.

THE BIBLE ATTRIBUTES OMNIPOTENCE TO GOD THE SON

The Bible attributes to the Son of God the same omnipotence that it declares of the Father. In many passages in the Gospels, we see how the Son of God had power over disease, how disease in all its forms was subject to His mere word. (See, for example, Luke 4:38–39; 17:12–14.) In still other passages, we see death subject to His word. (See, for example, Luke 7:14–15; 8:49–55; John 5:25.) In addition, we see how He had power over the elements, over the wind and sea, how they were subject to His word. (See Matthew 8:26–27; Mark 4:39–41.) He had power over the demons, also; they trembled at His presence and were subject to His word. We read in Matthew 8:16: *"When evening had come, they brought to Him many who were demon-possessed. And He cast out the spirits with a word, and healed all who were sick."* We read in Luke 4:35–36:

But Jesus rebuked him [the unclean demon in the man], *saying, "Be quiet, and come out of him!" And when the demon had thrown him in their midst, it came out of him and did not hurt him.*

And in Luke 4:41, we read: *"And demons also came out of many, crying out and saying, 'You are the Christ, the Son of God!' And He, rebuking them, did not allow them to speak."*

In Ephesians 1:20–22, we are told that all the heavenly hierarchies of angels are under Him and are subject to His word:

[God] *raised Him* [Jesus Christ] *from the dead and seated Him at His right hand in the heavenly places, far above all principality and power and might and dominion, and every name that is named, not only in this age but also in that which is to come. And He put all things under His feet, and gave Him to be head over all things to the church.*

Our Lord Jesus Himself said in Matthew 28:18, *"All authority has been given to Me in heaven and on earth."* And in Hebrews 1:3, we are told that the Son of God *"uphold*[s] *all things by the word of His power."*

THE BIBLE ATTRIBUTES OMNIPOTENCE TO THE SPIRIT

The Bible also tells us that omnipotence belongs to the third Person of the Trinity, the Holy Spirit. In announcing to the Virgin Mary the coming birth of her Son, the God-sent messenger said in Luke 1:35,

God Is Omnipotent

"The Holy Spirit will come upon you, and the power of the Highest will overshadow you; therefore, also, that Holy One who is to be born will be called the Son of God." In this verse, *"the power of the Highest"* that is, omnipotence, is ascribed to the Holy Spirit. And in the opening verses of the Bible, we read regarding the Holy Spirit:

> *In the beginning God created the heavens and the earth. The earth was without form, and void; and darkness was on the face of the deep. And the Spirit of God was hovering over the face of the waters. Then God said, "Let there be light"; and there was light.* (Gen. 1:1–3)

Oh, let us worship the wondrous triune God of the Bible—omnipotent Father; omnipotent Son, our Savior; and omnipotent Holy Spirit, our Sanctifier and Empowerer! What a marvelous God the God of the Bible is compared with the little gods of Theosophy, Christian Science, New Thought, Spiritualism, New Theology, modern philosophy, and all of the learned modern stupidity that is accepted by so many as philosophical profundity. Much that is called philosophy is merely *"grasping for the wind"* (Eccl. 2:17) and *"feed*[ing] *on the wind"* (Hos. 12:1).

GOD'S OMNIPOTENCE IS LIMITED ONLY BY HIS OWN WILL

Before we leave this inexhaustible subject of the omnipotence of God, one more thing should be said: The exercise of God's omnipotence is limited by His own wise, holy, and loving will.

God *can* do anything but *will* do only what infinite wisdom, holiness, and love dictate. This comes out in many places in the Bible. Read, for example, Isaiah 59:1–2:

> *Behold, the Lord's hand is not shortened, that it cannot save; nor His ear heavy, that it cannot hear. But your iniquities have separated you from your God; and your sins have hidden His face from you, so that He will not hear.*

The question is often asked, and it is a very natural question, "If God is omnipotent, why does He not destroy the Devil and bring his terrible work to an end?" If we could not answer this question, we could rest perfectly at peace in the thought that an infinitely wise God could easily have a thousand perfectly good reasons for doing or not doing something, when we in our finite foolishness could not see even one. But in this case, the answer to the question is simple and easy. God has not yet destroyed the Devil or put him out of business because, by his very maliciousness, he is working out part of God's benevolent purposes. God has purposes of love that are still to be worked out to a degree by the Devil's unintentional cooperation. For example, the Devil put it into the heart of Judas Iscariot to betray his Lord; but the Devil, by so doing, simply fulfilled God's prophecies of centuries before and confirmed the divine origin and inerrancy of the Book of God. Furthermore, the Devil, by so doing, led on to the atoning death of the Son of God, which meant salvation and pardon, justification and eternal life, sonship and coheirship with Jesus Christ for you and me.

God is omnipotent. He rules the universe. He rules heaven and earth. Yes, He rules Hades and hell also. Not one thing can be done by all the terrifying forces of misdirected nature, or by the most powerful men, or by angels or demons, or by the Devil himself, except by God's permission. Not one single demon can enter a pig except by the consent of the Son of God. (See Mark 5:1–13.) God rules the world, and therefore the ultimate outcome is sure: *"The Lord God Omnipotent reigns!"* (Rev. 19:6), and *"the kingdoms of this world* [will] *become the kingdoms of our Lord and of His Christ, and He shall reign forever and ever!"* (Rev. 11:15).

Chapter 7

GOD IS OMNISCIENT

Oh, the depth of the riches both of the wisdom and
knowledge of God! How unsearchable are His
judgments and His ways past finding out!
—Romans 11:33

I want to call your attention again to a very important and deeply significant fact that we have discovered in preceding chapters. The Bible, even in its earliest books, books written nearly thirty-four hundred years ago, presents a conception of God that is more profound, exalted, awe-inspiring, heartening, and delightful than can be found in all the profoundest philosophies of the past or even the present day—except insofar as the philosophies of the present day have formed their concepts of God from this old, old Book, the Bible.

We have also discovered that there is not to be found, in all the literature of all the nations and of all the ages, anything that even approaches the statements of the Bible in beauty, simplicity, grandeur, splendor, and sublimity of expression. And I call your attention again to the only explanation of these unquestionable facts that has even the slightest semblance of reasonableness. The Bible, even in its earliest portions, is a revelation from God, and these earliest writers of the Bible wrote the very words of Scripture as the Holy Spirit moved them, impelled them, and empowered them to write. Beyond any honest question, these earliest portions of the Holy Scriptures were really, as Paul declared they were, "God-breathed" (2 Tim. 3:16, literal Greek).

In the last chapter, we saw that God is omnipotent. He can do all things. The theme of this chapter is: God is omniscient. He knows all things. Let us begin by looking at seven Scriptures that illustrate this theme:

> *Listen to this, O Job; stand still and consider the wondrous works of God. Do you know when God dispatches them, and causes the light of His cloud to shine? Do you know how the clouds are balanced, those wondrous works of Him who is perfect in knowledge?*
> *(Job 37:14–16)*

> *He counts the number of the stars; He calls them all by name.* *(Ps. 147:4)*

> *Great is our Lord, and mighty in power; His understanding is infinite.* *(Ps. 147:5)*

> *If our heart condemns us, God is greater than our heart, and knows all things. (1 John 3:20)*

> *Are not two sparrows sold for a copper coin? And not one of them falls to the ground apart from your Father's will. But the very hairs of your head are all numbered. (Matt. 10:29–30)*

God Is Omniscient

Known to God from eternity are all His works.
(Acts 15:18)

Oh, the depth of the riches both of the wisdom
and knowledge of God! How unsearchable are
His judgments and His ways past finding out!
(Rom. 11:33)

GOD KNOWS ALL THINGS

Let me ask you to reflect on these passages for a long time. No mere cursory reading of them, no matter how simple, lucid, exact, and complete they may be, will enable you to take in all the marvelous wealth of meaning that there is in these brief but wondrous statements of God's Word. They must be pondered for a long time under the personal illumination of the Holy Spirit if we are to see and feel the glorious truth that is in them.

These passages, however, clearly teach us that God is *"perfect in knowledge"* (Job 37:16), that *"His understanding is infinite"* (Ps. 147:5), and that He *"knows all things"* (1 John 3:20). The Hebrew word translated *"perfect"* in Job 37:16 means "absolutely whole, entire, complete, finished, that to which nothing can be added." The thought is that, from all eternity, God's knowledge of all things is entire and complete, so that nothing whatsoever can ever be added to it. He knows everything about everything. He knows everything in all its height and depth and length and breadth, and in its every detail. There is nothing on earth or in heaven, nothing in those billions of inconceivably vast stars, nothing in the minutest of the most infinitesimal atoms or electrons of microscopic organisms and bacteria, which even the most powerful microscope cannot reveal, that God does not already fully know in its every detail.

How the astronomers of this century have labored and made discoveries that make the astronomy of earlier generations look like child's play! How the bacteriologists have perfected their techniques, and have dug and dug and dug, and discovered and discovered and discovered, until the most advanced bacteriology of earlier times now looks like kindergarten work! But God knew it all an eternity ago and knows infinitely more than either astronomers or bacteriologists have discovered even up to the present day. Our great God, Jehovah, is *"perfect in knowledge"* (Job 37:16).

The Hebrew word translated *"knowledge"* in this passage is in the plural and should be translated "knowledges." Therefore, the verse declares not only that God is *"perfect in knowledge"* but that He is "perfect in knowledges," that is, in all forms of knowledge. The same plural form is used in the Hebrew Bible, in 1 Samuel 2:3, in speaking of God: "Talk no more so exceeding proudly; let not arrogancy come out of thy mouth; for Jehovah is a God of knowledges."

Literally translated, the Hebrew words in Psalm 147:5 rendered *"His understanding is infinite"* would read, "To His insight (or "discernment," or "understanding") there is no number." In other words, God's insight is beyond all the measure and comprehension of finite beings.

SOME OF THE DETAILS OF WHAT GOD KNOWS

Now, these statements that we have considered so far regarding the infinite knowledge and omniscience of God are of a more or less general character.

God Is Omniscient

In order to appreciate and feel all the inspiration and glory of this great truth, we must go somewhat into detail, which the Bible itself does.

What are some of the details regarding His own omniscience that God reveals in the Bible?

God Sees Everything

First of all, let us look at Proverbs 15:3: *"The eyes of the LORD are in every place, keeping watch on the evil and the good."* Here we are told that God sees everything that occurs in every place and keeps *"watch on the evil and the good."* There is nothing that anyone does in any part of the universe, there is not the slightest act, good or evil, that God does not see and know and "keep watch on." We would all do well to keep this solemn fact in mind, day and night, and to remember that we cannot hide one thing we do from God, no matter how tightly we lock our doors against every intruder and how dark we make the room. As the psalmist expressed it in Psalm 139:11–12:

> *If I say, "Surely the darkness shall fall on me," even the night shall be light about me; indeed, the darkness shall not hide from You, but the night shines as the day; the darkness and the light are both alike to You.*

God Knows Everything in Creation

Second, let us look at two passages, one in the Psalms and one in Matthew—a statement of our Lord Jesus Himself—and put them together. The passage in the Psalms is Psalm 147:4: *"He counts the number of the stars; He calls them all by name."* The second passage is Matthew 10:29: *"Are not two sparrows sold for a copper coin? And not one of them falls to the ground apart from your Father's will."*

In these passages, we are told that God knows everything in creation, from the remotest stars in their inconceivably stupendous magnitude, down to the most insignificant bird in our gardens, the sparrow: *"not* [even] *one of them falls to the ground apart from your Father's will."*

God Knows the Ways and Works of Men

Third, let us turn to another passage from the Psalms and compare it with a verse from the book of Proverbs:

> *The LORD looks from heaven; He sees all the sons of men. From the place of His dwelling He looks on all the inhabitants of the earth; He fashions their hearts individually; He considers all their works.* (Ps. 33:13–15)

> *For the ways of man are before the eyes of the LORD, and He ponders all his paths.*
> (Prov. 5:21)

In the first passage, we are told that God *"sees all the sons of men"* and *"considers all their works."* In the second passage, we are told that *"the ways of man are before"* God's eyes and that *"He ponders* [*"maketh level,"* ASV] *all his paths* [*"goings,"* KJV]."

God Knows All Men's Deeds and Experiences

Fourth, we turn to still another psalm, Psalm 139:2–3:

God Is Omniscient

You know my sitting down and my rising up; You understand my thought afar off. You comprehend my path and my lying down, and are acquainted with all my ways.

Here we are told that God knows all men's deeds and experiences. Even the minutest and most insignificant details of our daily lives (our *"sitting down"* and our *"rising up"*) are known to God and are of interest to Him.

God Knows All Men's Words

Fifth, let us read the very next verse of Psalm 139: *"For there is not a word on my tongue, but behold, O LORD, You know it altogether"* (v. 4). In this verse, we are told that God knows all men's words. We do not ever speak a single word that God does not know and understand in all its aspects. You can deceive your fellowmen in your words, but you cannot deceive God.

We will return to this particular psalm. However, let me call your attention now to what a wonderful revelation of the omniscience and infinite wisdom of God we have in the Psalms, this old book of inspired songs, some of them written twenty-nine hundred years ago and all of them nearly that long ago. Where did the psalmists learn these wonderful truths so far beyond their time, so far beyond any time (including our own time) except insofar as men have learned them from the Bible? There is only one rational answer to this question, namely, that God supernaturally revealed these truths to them; the Psalms are God-breathed.

God Knows the Sorrows of His People

Sixth, let us look at a passage from the second book of the Bible, Exodus 3:7: *"And the LORD said: 'I have surely seen the oppression of My people who are in Egypt, and have heard their cry because of their taskmasters, for I know their sorrows.'"*

Here we are told that God knows the sorrows of His people. It often seems as if God does not know and does not care. It must have seemed so sometimes to Israel in Egypt. But God did know and God did care; and in due time, He proved that He knew and that He cared. It is the same way today. There is not a sorrow that any one of us experiences (no matter how hidden it may be from the eyes of men) that God does not know all about, and God cares. There is a tremendous amount of comfort and encouragement in this thought.

God Understands the Thoughts and Intents of Men

Seventh, let us return to Psalm 139: *"O LORD, You have searched me and known me. You know my sitting down and my rising up; You understand my thought afar off"* (vv. 1–2). Couple this with 1 Chronicles 28:9:

> *As for you, my son Solomon, know the God of your father, and serve Him with a loyal heart and with a willing mind; for the LORD searches all hearts and understands all the intent of the thoughts.*

From these two passages, we learn that God *"understands all the intent of the thoughts"* and that

He understands our thoughts *"afar off."* There is not one single thought or imagination in the minds of any one of us that God does not thoroughly understand, and He understands our thoughts even before we form them ourselves.

God Knows Even the Smallest Details of Men's Lives

Eighth, let us compare a verse from Psalm 139 with a statement of our Lord from Matthew 10:

You comprehend my path and my lying down, and are acquainted with all my ways.
(Ps. 139:3)

Are not two sparrows sold for a copper coin? And not one of them falls to the ground apart from your Father's will. But the very hairs of your head are all numbered. *(Matt. 10:29–30)*

In these two passages, we are brought face-to-face with the great truth that God's knowledge of us as individuals extends to the minutest particulars. He is *"acquainted with all* [our] *ways,"* and the *"very hairs of* [our] *head*[s] *are all numbered."* There is in these declarations of God's Word much food for reflection; there is in them both warning and comfort.

God Knows the End from the Beginning

Ninth, there is a remarkable passage regarding God's knowledge in Isaiah 46:9–10:

Remember the former things of old, for I am God, and there is no other; I am God, and

> *there is none like Me, declaring the end from*
> *the beginning, and from ancient times things*
> *that are not yet done.*   *(Isa. 46:9–10)*

Here we see that God knows from all eternity
what will be for all eternity. The same marvelous
truth is indicated in the New Testament, in 1 Peter
1:20, where we are told regarding Jesus Christ that
He *"was foreknown indeed before the foundation of*
the world, but was manifested at the end of the times
for your sake" (ASV).

God Knows from Eternity What Each Person Will Do

Tenth, the Bible goes beyond even these declarations in its detailed statements regarding the omniscience of God. It tells us over and over again that
God knows from the beginning what each individual
person will do. We see this fact, for example, in Matthew 20:17–19:

> *Now Jesus, going up to Jerusalem, took the*
> *twelve disciples aside on the road and said to*
> *them, "Behold, we are going up to Jerusalem,*
> *and the Son of Man will be betrayed to the*
> *chief priests and to the scribes; and they will*
> *condemn Him to death, and deliver Him to the*
> *Gentiles to mock and to scourge and to crucify.*
> *And the third day He will rise again."*

In this passage, our Lord Jesus declared with
minute detail exactly what various individuals were
going to do in connection with His own sufferings
and death. We find the same remarkable thought in
the Old Testament, in Exodus 3:19–20:

> *But I am sure that the king of Egypt will not*
> *let you go, no, not even by a mighty hand. So I*
> *will stretch out My hand and strike Egypt with*
> *all My wonders which I will do in its midst;*
> *and after that he will let you go.*
>
> *(Exod. 3:19–20)*

We see the same thing in 2 Kings 7:1–2, in a still more remarkable passage. It reveals the detailed knowledge of God regarding what each individual will do and what each individual will experience in the future.

> *Then Elisha said, "Hear the word of the*
> *LORD. Thus says the LORD: 'Tomorrow about*
> *this time a seah of fine flour shall be sold for a*
> *shekel, and two seahs of barley for a shekel, at*
> *the gate of Samaria.'" So an officer on whose*
> *hand the king leaned answered the man of*
> *God and said, "Look, if the LORD would make*
> *windows in heaven, could this thing be?" And*
> *he said, "In fact, you shall see it with your*
> *eyes, but you shall not eat of it."*
>
> *(2 Kings 7:1–2)*

In Psalm 41:9, we see the action of Judas Iscariot in the betrayal of his Lord, foreknown by God and definitely predicted a thousand years before it was actually done: *"Even my own familiar friend in whom I trusted, who ate my bread, has lifted up his heel against me."*

Paul declared the same fact regarding God's knowledge of himself in Galatians 1:15–16:

> *But when it pleased God, who separated me*
> *from my mother's womb and called me*

through His grace, to reveal His Son in me,
that I might preach Him among the Gentiles, I
did not immediately confer with flesh and
blood.   *(Gal. 1:15–16)*

And in 1 Peter 1:2, the same thing is declared regarding God's knowledge of each one of the elect:

Elect according to the foreknowledge of God
the Father, in sanctification of the Spirit, for
obedience and sprinkling of the blood of Jesus
Christ: grace to you and peace be multiplied.

One of the theories that is most fixed and immovable in the minds of the so-called modern biblical scholars, the modern critical scholars, the self-styled "historical school of biblical interpretation" (though its methods are in reality utterly unhistorical and unscientific), is that there is not a possibility of any such thing as detailed prediction in the Bible. Yet this theory completely loses sight of two firmly established facts, each of them not only taught in the Bible but also demonstrated by the indisputable facts in the case: first, that God is omniscient; second, that the Bible, in all its parts, is a revelation from this omniscient God. If it were not for the deep-seated prejudice of the natural heart against all things that are truly of a spiritual nature, these self-confident "modern biblical scholars" would be the laughingstock of all fair-minded, really intelligent, and clear-seeing men. They are rendered ridiculous by the clearly demonstrated facts in the case. But facts have no weight with these dreamers. Theories are the only things that interest them; and if the facts do not agree with the theories, so much the worse for the facts.

God Knows from Eternity the Whole Plan of the Ages

Finally, the Bible teaches us that God knows from all eternity the whole plan of the ages and each person's part in that plan. We are told this time and time again. For example, in Ephesians 1:9–12, we read:

> *Having made known to us the mystery of His will, according to His good pleasure which He purposed in Himself, that in the dispensation of the fullness of the times He might gather together in one all things in Christ, both which are in heaven and which are on earth; in Him. In Him also we have obtained an inheritance, being predestined according to the purpose of Him who works all things according to the counsel of His will, that we who first trusted in Christ should be to the praise of His glory.*

Also, in Ephesians 3:3–11, we read:

> *By revelation He made known to me [Paul] the mystery (as I have briefly written already, by which, when you read, you may understand my knowledge in the mystery of Christ), which in other ages was not made known to the sons of men, as it has now been revealed by the Spirit to His holy apostles and prophets: that the Gentiles should be fellow heirs, of the same body, and partakers of His promise in Christ*

through the gospel, of which I became a minister according to the gift of the grace of God given to me by the effective working of His power. To me, who am less than the least of all the saints, this grace was given, that I should preach among the Gentiles the unsearchable riches of Christ, and to make all see what is the fellowship of the mystery, which from the beginning of the ages has been hidden in God who created all things through Jesus Christ; to the intent that now the manifold wisdom of God might be made known by the church to the principalities and powers in the heavenly places, according to the eternal purpose which He accomplished in Christ Jesus our Lord.

(Eph. 3:3–11)

We find the same truth again more briefly expressed in Colossians 1:25–26:

I [Paul] *became a minister according to the stewardship from God which was given to me for you, to fulfill the word of God, the mystery which has been hidden from ages and from generations, but now has been revealed to His saints.*

We see clearly in these passages that the whole plan of the ages and each person's part in it has been known to God from all eternity. There are no afterthoughts with God. He knows and plans everything from the beginning. Well may we exclaim, *"Oh, the depth of the riches both of the wisdom and knowledge of God! How unsearchable are His judgments and His ways past finding out!"* (Rom. 11:33).

God Is Omniscient

Before we leave this inexhaustible subject of the omniscience of God as it is set forth in the Bible, let me call your attention to the fact that the same omniscience that is attributed to God the Father is also attributed to Jesus Christ the Son and to the Holy Spirit.

We see this truth in regard to our Lord Jesus over and over again. We observe, for example, in John 4:16–19, that Jesus knew people's lives, even their secret histories. We see that Jesus knew the secret thoughts of men (Mark 2:8; Luke 5:22), that *"He knew all men"* (John 2:24), and that *"He knew what was in man"* (v. 25).

In addition, we read in John 6:64 that Jesus knew from the beginning that Judas would betray Him. John said, *"Jesus knew from the beginning who they were who did not believe, and who would betray Him."* Not only men's present thoughts but also their future choices were all known to Him. Simon Peter specifically declared in John 21:17 that Jesus knew *"all things,"* and the whole company of disciples professed in John 16:30, *"Now we are sure that You know all things."* Paul declared in Colossians 2:3 that in Christ *"are hidden all the treasures of wisdom and knowledge."* The fact that the Holy Spirit also is omniscient, that He knows all things, is plainly declared in 1 Corinthians 2:10–11, John 14:26, and John 16:12–13.

O wondrous and glorious triune God of the Bible, God the Father, God the Son, and God the Holy Spirit! You know all things. You are *"perfect in knowledge"* (Job 37:16), and Your *"understanding is infinite"* (Ps. 147:5). We worship You, we rejoice in You, and we rest in You, knowing that You will never be taken by surprise or meet any emergency that You have not foreknown from all eternity and for which You are not fully prepared. We do not know the future, but You do. Things look very dark to us and full of foreboding and overwhelming disaster in business, in politics, and in international affairs. But You have known all these present perils from all eternity and have fully provided for them all; therefore, we know that the ultimate outcome (however dark the present outlook may seem) will be full of blessing and glory. Hallelujah! Surely it *"is eternal life* [to] *know You, the only true God, and Jesus Christ whom You have sent"* (John 17:3). Glorious God of the Bible!

Chapter 8

GOD IS HOLY

The LORD our God is holy.
—Psalm 99:9

I n the preceding chapters, we have seen that in the Bible, even in its earliest books, books written nearly thirty-four hundred years ago, a conception of God is presented to us that is more profound, more exalted, more awe-inspiring, and more delightful, heart-thrilling, and ennobling than can be found in any or all of the profoundest philosophies of the past or even the present day—except insofar as the philosophies of the present day have borrowed their ideas of God from the Bible.

We have also seen that there is not to be found in all the literature of all nations and of all ages, anything that even approaches the statements of the Bible in beauty, simplicity, grandeur, splendor, and sublimity of expression. And we have seen that the only explanation for these two unquestionable facts that has even the slightest semblance of reasonableness is that the Bible, even in its earliest portions, is a direct and supernatural revelation from God. The earliest writers of the Bible, as well as the later writers, wrote the very words that are found in the Holy Scriptures as the Holy Spirit moved them, impelled them, and empowered them to write. Beyond the possibility of any intelligent and honest question, the earliest portions of the Holy Scriptures were indeed—as Paul more than eighteen hundred fifty years ago declared them to be—"God-breathed" (1 Tim. 3:16, literal Greek).

But it is only when we consider the moral character of God that we see, to the full extent, the immeasurable superiority of the conception of God that the Bible presents to all representations of God found elsewhere. Therefore, starting in this chapter, we will study the moral character of the God of the Bible.

THE HOLINESS OF GOD

First, we will see that the Bible declares that God is holy. I have chosen ten Scripture texts that clearly demonstrate this truth. The first text comes from one of the earlier books of the Bible, the book of Joshua. This book is nearly as old as the oldest books in the Bible, for Joshua was, for a large part of his life, a contemporary of Moses.

> *Joshua said to the people, "You cannot serve the LORD, for He is a holy God. He is a jealous God; He will not forgive your transgressions nor your sins."* (Josh. 24:19)

> *You are holy, enthroned in the praises of Israel.* (Ps. 22:3)

God Is Holy

Exalt the LORD our God, and worship at His footstool; He is holy....Exalt the LORD our God, and worship at His holy hill; for the LORD our God is holy. (Ps. 99:5, 9)

The LORD of hosts shall be exalted in judgment, and God who is holy shall be hallowed in righteousness. (Isa. 5:16)

In the year that King Uzziah died, I [Isaiah] saw the Lord sitting on a throne, high and lifted up, and the train of His robe filled the temple. Above it stood seraphim; each one had six wings: with two he covered his face, with two he covered his feet, and with two he flew. And one cried to another and said: "Holy, holy, holy is the LORD of hosts; the whole earth is full of His glory!" (Isa. 6:1–3)

For thus says the High and Lofty One who inhabits eternity, whose name is Holy: "I dwell in the high and holy place, with him who has a contrite and humble spirit, to revive the spirit of the humble, and to revive the heart of the contrite ones." (Isa. 57:15)

[The night before His crucifixion, Jesus prayed,] *"Now I am no longer in the world, but these are in the world, and I come to You. Holy Father, keep through Your name those whom You have given Me, that they may be one as We are."* (John 17:11)

As He who called you is holy, you also be holy in all your conduct, because it is written, "Be holy, for I am holy." (1 Pet. 1:15–16)

Therefore, since we are receiving a kingdom which cannot be shaken, let us have grace, by which we may serve God acceptably with reverence and godly fear. For our God is a consuming fire. (Heb. 12:28–29)

This is the message which we have heard from Him and declare to you, that God is light and in Him is no darkness at all. (1 John 1:5)

In eight of these ten passages from the Bible, the plain and direct declaration is made that God is holy, and the ninth and tenth texts set forth this same great truth in remarkably significant and indicative ways. The tenth text contains one of the most illuminating and awe-inspiring sentences ever written: *"God is light and in Him is no darkness at all."* These words present the truth that God is not only holy but that He is *absolutely* holy. *"In Him is no darkness at all."*

Isaiah 57:15 also deserves special notice: *"For thus says the High and Lofty One who inhabits eternity, whose name is Holy."* In this verse, we are told that God's *"name is Holy."* Now, in the Bible, a name stands for the revealed character of a person. So the words *"[God's] name is Holy"* mean that holiness is the essential moral nature of God. *Holy* is what Jehovah, the God of the Bible, is in His innermost, essential moral being. Jehovah, the God of the Bible, is called *"the Holy One"* over twenty-five times in the book of Isaiah. He is also called this in both Jeremiah and Ezekiel, and elsewhere as well.

In the New Testament, God the Son is spoken of as *"the Holy One"* (see, for example, Mark 1:24;

Luke 1:35; Acts 2:27), and the third Person of the Trinity is constantly spoken of as *"the Holy Spirit."* (See, for example, Matthew 3:11; Luke 3:22; Acts 2:4.) The whole Bible, both the Old Testament and the New, is dominated by one thought: the infinite holiness of God.

What Does "Holy" Mean?

This brings us to the important question, What does the word *holy* mean, according to the Bible? This question is plainly answered in many places in the Scriptures. Let me give you two illustrative examples that anyone can easily understand. The first is found in Leviticus 11:43–45:

> *You shall not make yourselves abominable with any creeping thing that creeps; nor shall you make yourselves unclean with them, lest you be defiled by them. For I am the LORD your God. You shall therefore consecrate yourselves, and you shall be holy; for I am holy. Neither shall you defile yourselves with any creeping thing that creeps on the earth. For I am the LORD who brings you up out of the land of Egypt, to be your God. You shall therefore be holy, for I am holy.*

It is evident from these words that *holy* means to be free from all defilement, to be absolutely pure. The words *God is holy* mean that God is absolutely pure. The same thought is set forth in a little different way in Deuteronomy 23:14:

> *For the LORD your God walks in the midst of your camp, to deliver you and give your enemies*

*over to you; therefore your camp shall be holy,
that He may see no unclean thing among you,
and turn away from you.   (Deut. 23:14)*

The meaning of the word *holiness*, as well as the truth that God is absolutely and infinitely holy, are set forth in what is perhaps the highest expression of the great truth of the infinite holiness of God that is to be found in the Bible, a passage to which I have already referred, 1 John 1:5: *"God is light and in Him is no darkness at all."*

The instructions for living, working, worshipping, and approaching God that the Lord gave to His people Israel in the Old Testament, as well as the experiences of the Israelites, were intended to teach, emphasize, and burn into their minds and hearts the fundamental truth, the great foundational truth, that God is holy, unapproachably holy. Some of these were: the entire Mosaic system of washings; the divisions of the tabernacle; the division of the people into ordinary Israelites, Levites, ordinary priests, and high priests, who were permitted different degrees of approach to God under strictly defined conditions; the insistence upon sacrifice with the shedding of blood and the giving up of the life of the substitute sacrifice as the one always necessary medium of approach to God; God's directions to Moses in Exodus 3:5, *"Do not draw near this place. Take your sandals off your feet, for the place where you stand is holy ground,"* and to Joshua in Joshua 5:15: *"Take your sandal off your foot, for the place where you stand is holy"*; the punishment of Uzziah (2 Chron. 26:12–23); the strict orders to Israel in regard to approaching Sinai when Jehovah came down upon it (Exod. 19:9–13); the doom of Korah, Dathan, and Abiram because of their presumption in approaching God in their own way (Num. 16:1–33); and the destruction of Nadab and Abihu because they dared to draw near to God in another way than He had prescribed (Lev. 10:1–2).

The truth that God is holy is the one great foundational truth of the Bible—of both the Old Testament and the New, of the Jewish religion and of the Christian religion.

MANIFESTATIONS OF THE HOLINESS OF GOD

Now let us look at what the Bible teaches us regarding how the holiness of God is manifested.

God Has an Intense Hatred of Sin

First of all, the holiness of God manifests itself in an intense hatred of sin. This is set forth in Habakkuk 1:12–13:

Are You not from everlasting, O LORD my God, my Holy One? We shall not die. O LORD, You have appointed them for judgment; O Rock, You have marked them for correction. You are of purer eyes than to behold evil, and cannot look on wickedness.

We see the same great truth presented in the very first book in the Bible, in Genesis 6:5–7:

And Jehovah saw that the wickedness of man was great in the earth, and that every imagination of the thoughts of his heart was only

> *evil continually. And it repented Jehovah that*
> *he had made man on the earth, and it grieved*
> *him at his heart. And Jehovah said, I will de-*
> *stroy man whom I have created from the face*
> *of the ground.*   *(Gen. 6:5–7 ASV)*

It was the infinite holiness of God, His intense hatred
of sin, that necessitated the Flood when the human
race had become incurably bad. And so the Adamic
race as a whole, with the exception of Noah and his
family, was destroyed, and a new beginning was
made.

The same truth is set forth in Deuteronomy
25:16, *"For all who do such things, all who behave*
unrighteously, are an abomination to the LORD your
God," and in Proverbs 15:9, 26, where Solomon declared that both *"the way of the wicked"* and *"the*
thoughts of the wicked" are *"an abomination to the*
LORD."

God Has an Intense Delight in Holiness

In the second place, the holiness of God manifests itself in intense delight in righteousness and
holiness. We will look at just one passage that is illustrative of this thought. It is the last half of Proverbs 15:9, one of the verses we just looked at: *"The*
way of the wicked is an abomination to the LORD, but
He loves him who follows righteousness."

Sin in all its forms moves the holy heart of Jehovah with intense loathing, but righteousness, on
the other hand, moves the holy heart of Jehovah
with intense joy and delight.

In Leviticus 20:26, Jehovah told Israel that He
had separated them from all other people for the

express purpose that they should be *"holy to [Him]"* and, by being holy, be His very own: *"That you should be Mine."*

God Never Does Wickedness

In the third place, the holiness of God manifests itself in His never doing wickedness or iniquity. This thought is set forth in the inspired message of Elihu as recorded in Job 34:10: *"Therefore listen to me, you men of understanding: far be it from God to do wickedness, and from the Almighty to commit iniquity."*

God Must Separate Sinners from Himself

In the fourth place, the holiness of God is manifested in the separation of the sinner from Himself. This thought is given in a passage in Isaiah that is very familiar to us all, Isaiah 59:1–2:

Behold, the Lord's hand is not shortened, that it cannot save; nor His ear heavy, that it cannot hear. But your iniquities have separated you from your God; and your sins have hidden His face from you, so that He will not hear.

It is because of this necessary manifestation of the holiness of the true God—separating the sinner from Himself because His holiness requires it—that an atonement by the shedding of the blood of a sufficient Substitute was necessary if there was to be any approach to God on the part of the sinner. This great fundamental truth is set forth in Ephesians 2:13, *"But now in Christ Jesus you who once were far off have been brought near by the blood of Christ,"* and in Hebrews 10:10, *"By that will* [the will of God] *we have been sanctified through the offering of the body of Jesus Christ once for all."*

Our Lord's own words set forth the same fundamental truth. He said, *"The Son of Man did not come to be served, but to serve, and to give His life a ransom for many"* (Matt. 20:28), and *"I am the way, the truth, and the life. No one comes to the Father except through Me"* (John 14:6).

All approach to a holy God (such as the God of the Bible is) on the part of sinful men (such as we all are) must be on the ground of shed blood. The atonement that our Lord Jesus Christ made by His death on the cross had its first and deepest demand in the holiness of God. Any doctrine of the Atonement that considers the Atonement necessary only so that men may be influenced by a powerful motive (the so-called "Moral Influence Theory of the Atonement") or for producing moral conduct (the so-called "Governmental Theory of the Atonement") does not go to the root of things. The first and fundamental reason why *"without shedding of blood there is no remission* [of sins]*"* (Heb. 9:22) is that God is holy and sin must be covered before there can be fellowship between God and the sinner. Nothing can cover sin from the holy gaze and the intense disapproval of God except the atoning blood of Jesus Christ.

God Must Punish Sin

In the fifth place, the holiness of God manifests itself in the punishment of the sinner. The Bible declares this over and over again in direct and explicit statements and by illustrative examples. Let us look at three such passages:

*And the LORD passed before him and pro-
claimed, "The LORD, the LORD God, merciful
and gracious, longsuffering, and abounding
in goodness and truth, keeping mercy for thousands, forgiving iniquity and transgression
and sin, by no means clearing the guilty, visiting the iniquity of the fathers upon the children and the children's children to the third
and the fourth generation."* (Exod. 34:6–7)

*And Jehovah saw that the wickedness of man
was great in the earth, and that every imagination of the thoughts of his heart was only
evil continually. And it repented Jehovah that
he had made man on the earth, and it grieved
him at his heart. And Jehovah said, I will destroy man whom I have created from the face
of the ground; both man, and beast, and creeping things, and birds of the heavens; for it re-
penteth me that I have made them.*
(Gen. 6:5–7 ASV)

*For You are not a God who takes pleasure in
wickedness, nor shall evil dwell with You. The
boastful shall not stand in Your sight; You
hate all workers of iniquity. You shall destroy
those who speak falsehood; the LORD abhors
the bloodthirsty and deceitful man.* (Ps. 5:4–6)

According to the Bible (and according to reason
and common sense), God does not punish the sinner
merely for the sinner's own good. God punishes the
sinner because God is a *holy* Being and therefore
hates sin. God's holiness, His hatred of sin, like
every attribute of His, is real. It is a living thing; it is

153

active and not dormant, and must manifest itself. God's holy wrath at sin must strike. This truth is set forth in a remarkable way in Isaiah 53:6. Let me give you a literal translation of the Hebrew: "All we like sheep have gone astray; we have turned every one to his own way; and Jehovah has made to strike on him the iniquity of us all."

Any view of the punishment of sin that leaves out the thought that it is an expression of God's holy hatred of sin is not only unbiblical but is also shallow and dishonoring to God. God is holy, infinitely holy; therefore, He infinitely hates sin. We ourselves, in our own feelings, get a glimpse at times of what God's holy hatred of sin must be in our own burning indignation at some enormous iniquity. But we must remember that God is *infinitely* holy, and therefore God's wrath at the smallest sin is infinitely greater than ours is at the greatest moral outrage. It is true, as we will see later, that God is love; but God's love is not of the sickly, sentimental sort, the morally putrid sort, that sends costly bouquets and tender letters to moral monsters. No, thank God! *"Our God is a consuming fire"* (Heb. 12:29). God's love toward sinners will never be understood and appreciated until it is seen in the white light of His blazing wrath at sin.

God Saves Us from Sin to Bring Us into Holiness

Sixth, we come now to the most amazing and most decisive manifestation of the holiness of God. The holiness of God manifested itself in His making an infinite sacrifice to save others from sin, which He hates, and to bring them into holiness, which He loves. Let me give you just two passages from the Word of God that set forth this greatest thought of all regarding the way in which God's holiness is manifested. We owe this thought entirely to the Bible. There is not the slightest suggestion of it from all the philosophers, poets, thinkers, and mystics of all nations and of all the ages (except as they have borrowed it from the Bible). The first passage is one of the most familiar verses in the Bible, John 3:16: *"For God so loved the world that He gave His only begotten Son, that whoever believes in Him should not perish but have everlasting life."* The second passage is 1 Peter 3:18: *"Christ also suffered once for sins, the just for the unjust, that He might bring us to God."*

The death of Jesus Christ on the cross of Calvary was not merely a manifestation of the amazing and infinite *love* of God; it was also a manifestation of the amazing and infinite *holiness* of God. This fact comes out in the little word *"so"* in John 3:16: *"God so loved the world that He gave His only begotten Son, that whoever believes in Him should not perish but have everlasting life."* That word *"so"* not only sets forth the greatness of God's love, in that it did not draw back even from the sacrifice of His very best, His only begotten Son, to save us, but also sets forth the quality of His love. It was a holy love, a love that would not and could not pardon sin, which was infinitely hateful to God, until sin had been atoned for and covered from His holy gaze by atoning blood—even the blood of the Son of His eternal love. I leave this amazing truth to each one of you to ponder and marvel over. Let us worship God for His immeasurable grace.

The God of the Bible

IMPLICATIONS OF THE TRUTH THAT GOD IS HOLY

Let me now call your attention to some inferences of immense practical importance from the great fundamental truth that God is holy, that *"God is light and in Him is no darkness at all"* (1 John 1:5).

We Must Come to God with Awe

First, we must draw near to God with awe. This thought is set forth time and time again in the Bible. For example, we read in Hebrews 12:28–29:

> *Therefore, since we are receiving a kingdom which cannot be shaken, let us have grace, by which we may serve God acceptably with reverence and godly fear. For our God is a consuming fire.*

We also see this truth in the Old Testament, in Exodus 3:4–5:

> *So when the LORD saw that* [Moses] *turned aside to look, God called to him from the midst of the bush and said, "Moses, Moses!" And he said, "Here I am." Then* [God] *said, "Do not draw near this place. Take your sandals off your feet, for the place where you stand is holy ground."*

Perhaps the most remarkable passage that sets forth this truth that Jehovah, the God of the Bible, is of such a nature that we must draw near to Him with awe, is Isaiah 6:1–3:

In the year that King Uzziah died, I saw the Lord sitting on a throne, high and lifted up, and the train of His robe filled the temple. Above it stood seraphim; each one had six wings: with two he covered his face, with two he covered his feet, and with two he flew. And one cried to another and said: "Holy, holy, holy is the LORD of hosts; the whole earth is full of His glory!" (Isa. 6:1–3)

In this passage, we see that even the holy *"seraphim"* (*seraphim* is Hebrew for "burning ones," that is, burning in their own intense holiness) covered their faces and their feet in Jehovah's presence. They had four wings for worship but only two for service. Of course, we who are in Christ Jesus have a place above the seraphim, for when Jesus Christ died on the cross, He took our place, the place of rejection before God. The very moment that we accept Jesus Christ, we step into His place of perfect acceptance before God. Therefore, we have a right to come into God's presence with uncovered faces and to look up into His face with perfect childlike confidence and call Him "Father." Nevertheless, we should never lose sight of the fact that while God is our Father, He is our *"Holy Father"* (John 17:11); and so, along with our fearless, childlike trust, there should also be a profound sense of awe in the presence of this infinitely holy Being whom we call "God" and "Father." The light and frivolous way, the careless and familiar way, with which many Christians, both ministers and laypeople, draw near to God today in what they call prayer and praise and worship, is shocking to anyone who has any real and complete biblical conception of who and what God is. God is *holy*. Never forget that when you draw near to Him.

God's Holiness Reveals Our Sinfulness

The second important inference from the fact that God is infinitely holy is that the pure light of God's holiness reveals the blackness of our own sinfulness. We see this in a verse that follows almost immediately after those we read from Isaiah in the last section:

> So I said: "Woe is me, for I am undone! Because I am a man of unclean lips, and I dwell in the midst of a people of unclean lips; for my eyes have seen the King, the LORD of hosts."
>
> (Isa. 6:5)

Isaiah, who spoke these words, was perhaps the holiest man of his day. But when he came to the place where he actually met God, the undimmed, dazzling white light of the infinite holiness of God revealed to him the depths of his own vileness and led him to cry out, *"Woe is me, for I am undone! Because I am a man of unclean lips, and I dwell in the midst of a people of unclean lips."*

We see the same thing in Job 42:5–6. Job had been firmly maintaining his own perfect and unblemished integrity against all the accusations and insinuations of his friends, but then he came face-to-face with God Himself, the infinitely holy One, and he cried out, *"I have heard of You by the hearing of the ear, but now my eye sees You. Therefore I abhor myself, and repent in dust and ashes."*

If anyone thinks well of himself, he has never met God. Nothing will demolish self-righteousness like one real sight of God.

God Is Holy

If there could burst upon us one glimpse of God as He really is in His infinite holiness, as He is as the seraphim behold Him in heaven right now, every one of us would fall on his face before God and cry out, *"Woe is me, for I am undone! Because I am a man of unclean lips, and I dwell in the midst of a people of unclean lips"* (Isa. 6:5) and *"God, be merciful to me a sinner!"* (Luke 18:13).

There Is No Forgiveness without Atonement

The third great and necessary inference from the fact that God is infinitely holy is that there is no forgiveness without atonement. This all-important truth is declared over and over again in many different ways in the Old Testament and also in the New Testament. One illustration of this fact is enough: *"Without shedding of blood there is no remission* [of sins]" (Heb. 9:22).

Sin must be covered from the holy gaze of God, and nothing will cover it but the blood of Christ Jesus. Let me ask you, Is your sin covered?

This great truth that there is no forgiveness without atonement runs all through the Bible and determines very much of both its history and its explicit teaching. Way back in the Garden of Eden, when sin first entered human history, Adam and Eve tried to cover their sin and their shame with self-made garments of leaves. But God covered them with the skins taken from animals *whose blood had been shed,* who were types of the atonement of Jesus Christ. Soon after that, Cain and Abel came to God with their sacrifices. (See Genesis 4:3–4.) Cain came bearing the fair and fragrant fruits of the ground, but was not allowed to approach God. Abel came with the shed blood of the firstborn of his flock, and *"the LORD respected Abel and his offering, but He did not respect Cain and his offering"* (Gen. 4:4–5).

What do those stern judgments upon sin that are recorded in the Old Testament mean—the blotting out of the whole ancient world by the Flood; the blotting out of the Canaanites, men, women, and children; God's stern judgments upon Israel; and all the appalling judgments of the Bible? They mean that God is holy and hates sin.

What does that constant, ever flowing river of blood that runs through the entire Old Testament mean, beginning in the garden of Eden when sin first entered and ever widening—the blood of thousands, yes, millions of innocent lambs and other sacrificial animals? It means that God is holy, that man is a sinner, and that *"without shedding of blood there is no remission* [of sins]" (Heb. 9:22).

What does that supreme tragedy of all history, the tragedy of Calvary, mean? There the only perfectly holy and righteous Man who ever walked this earth hung dying on a cross, with a robber on a cross at each side and the mob mocking *Him* and not the robbers. This Man was not only deserted by men but also by God, and He cried out with a breaking heart, *"My God, My God, why have You forsaken Me?"* (Matt. 27:46). What does it mean, this profoundest of all the mysteries of all the ages? It means that God is holy, that man is a sinner, and that *"without shedding of blood* [and thus the making of a perfect atonement] *there is no remission* [of sins]."

The Wonderfulness of God's Love

The fourth inference from the fact of the infinite holiness of God is the wonderfulness of God's love. It would be no wonder if an unholy God could love unholy men. But that the God *"whose name is Holy"* (Isa. 57:15), the God who is absolutely holy, the God who has holiness for His essential moral nature, the infinitely holy God, could love beings so utterly sinful as we are, that is the wonder of the eternities. There are many deep mysteries in the Bible, but none other as profound as this.

Chapter 9

GOD IS LOVE

And we have known and believed the love
that God has for us. God is love.
—1 John 4:16

We have learned that it is only when we come to a consideration of the moral character of God that we see, to the fullest extent, the immeasurable superiority of the conception of God that the Bible presents, compared with all representations of God found in the profoundest philosophies of the past or the present, or in the literature of all nations and of all ages. We have also seen that the only reasonable explanation for this superior conception of God is that the Scriptures, as the apostle Paul more than eighteen hundred fifty years ago declared them to be, are "God-breathed" (2 Tim. 3:16, literal Greek).

In the last chapter, we began our study of the moral character of God, beginning with the foundational fact that God is holy, infinitely and absolutely holy, that *"God is light and in Him is no darkness at all"* (1 John 1:5).

But the same book of the Bible that contains that wondrous statement, *"God is light and in Him is no darkness at all,"* one of the most illuminating and awe-inspiring sentences ever written, contains another sentence that is perhaps *the* greatest sentence ever written: *"God is love"* (1 John 4:8, 16). This great theme is the topic of this chapter.

I have tried to keep my Scripture texts to as small a number as possible. Even so, I am compelled, by the very breadth of the topic, to include twelve texts. I will also be compelled, as we go on, to introduce numerous other passages of Scripture, if we are to treat this great subject with anything like fullness and fairness. Please take careful note of these Scripture texts, for the whole message of the chapter is in my texts. It is the God of the Bible that we are studying, not the God of my thoughts or my philosophy or my theology anymore than the god of modern philosophy or the god of New Theology. All we know about God that is really worthwhile is what this one Book teaches.

It would be amusing, if it were not righteously exasperating, to hear our meager-minded but very self-sufficient modern philosophers and theologians say, "I *think* so and so about God." Who cares what you think? Who cares what I think? The only thing of any real importance is: What does God Himself reveal about Himself in the one Book that is the only God-breathed revelation of God? What does the Bible say? That is the only thing that really matters. Therefore, this entire chapter contains only an exposition of what God Himself clearly and plainly says in His own Book. And this is what He says:

> He who does not love does not know God, for
> God is love.   *(1 John 4:8)*

God Is Love

*And we have known and believed the love that
God has for us. God is love, and he who abides
in love abides in God, and God in him.*
(1 John 4:16)

*Beloved, let us love one another, for love is of
God; and everyone who loves is born of God
and knows God.* *(1 John 4:7)*

*By this we know love, because He laid down
His life for us. And we also ought to lay down
our lives for the brethren. But whoever has this
world's goods, and sees his brother in need,
and shuts up his heart from him, how does the
love of God abide in him?* *(1 John 3:16–17)*

*Father, I desire that they also whom You gave
Me may be with Me where I am, that they may
behold My glory which You have given Me; for
You loved Me before the foundation of the
world.* *(John 17:24)*

*For God so loved the world that He gave His
only begotten Son, that whoever believes in
Him should not perish but have everlasting
life.* *(John 3:16)*

*For when we were still without strength, in
due time Christ died for the ungodly. For
scarcely for a righteous man will one die; yet
perhaps for a good man someone would even
dare to die. But God demonstrates His own
love toward us, in that while we were still sinners, Christ died for us.* *(Rom. 5:6–8)*

*But God, who is rich in mercy, because of His
great love with which He loved us, even when*

*we were dead in trespasses, made us alive to-
gether with Christ (by grace you have been
saved).*   *(Eph. 2:4–5)*

*In this the love of God was manifested toward
us, that God has sent His only begotten Son
into the world, that we might live through
Him. In this is love, not that we loved God, but
that He loved us and sent His Son to be the
propitiation for our sins.*   *(1 John 4:9–10)*

*But I say to you, **love your enemies**...and pray
for those who spitefully use you and persecute
you, **that you may be sons of your Father in
heaven**; for He makes His sun rise on the evil
and on the good, and sends rain on the just
and on the unjust.*

(Matt. 5:44–45, emphasis added)

*The LORD your God in your midst, the Mighty
One, will save; He will rejoice over you with
gladness, He will quiet you with His love, He
will rejoice over you with singing. (Zeph. 3:17)*

*In the beginning God created the heavens and
the earth. The earth was without form, and
void; and darkness was on the face of the deep.
And the Spirit of God was hovering over the
face of the waters. Then God said, "Let there
be light"; and there was light....Then God
said, "**Let Us make man in Our image**, according to Our likeness; let them have dominion over the fish of the sea, over the birds of the
air, and over the cattle, over all the earth and
over every creeping thing that creeps on the*

*earth." **So God created man in His own image; in the image of God He created him; male and female He created them.** Then God blessed them, and God said to them, "Be fruitful and multiply; fill the earth and subdue it; have dominion over the fish of the sea, over the birds of the air, and over every living thing that moves on the earth."...Then God saw everything that He had made, and indeed it was very good. (Gen. 1:1–3, 26–28, 31, emphasis added)*

THE INFINITE LOVE OF GOD

In the first two texts, we are told in so many words that *"God is love"* (1 John 4:8, 16). The other texts imply the same great truth. More of the texts are taken from John's writings—either his gospel or his first epistle—than from any other writer. However, some of the most notable texts are taken from Paul's writings, one is from the words of our Lord Jesus Himself, one is from one of the least-studied Old Testament prophets, and one consists of several verses from the very first chapter in the Bible, written about thirty-four hundred years ago. These verses all set forth the tremendous and stupendous truth that God is love. It is not merely that God loves, but that God *is* love. In other words, love is the very essence of His moral nature. He is also the source of all love.

The whole Bible is a love story, the story of the infinite love of an infinitely holy God for a fallen and morally worthless race of sinners, of which you and I are members. If anyone were to ask me to suggest a sentence to print in gold letters on the cover of his

Bible, a sentence that would summarize the entire contents of the Book, it would be that most marvelous sentence ever written, consisting of only three monosyllables and only nine letters: *"God is love."*

I said in the last chapter that the whole Bible, both the Old Testament and the New, is dominated by one thought: the infinite holiness of God. This statement is equally true: The whole Bible, both the Old Testament and the New, is dominated by one thought, the thought that God is love, that love is the very essence of God's moral nature.

WHAT DOES "LOVE" MEAN?

This brings us to the important question, What does the word *love* mean, or what is love? We must go to the Bible itself for a satisfying and entirely dependable answer to this all-important question. This is the point at which a multitude of preachers, theologians, poets, dreamers, and founders of various cults have gone astray; they have taken from the Bible the great truth that God is love, and then have not been wise enough and fair-minded enough to search the Bible to find out exactly how God Himself defines or describes love. Consequently, they have drawn all sorts of unwarranted conclusions from the statement that "God is love" and have fallen into all sorts of entirely unbiblical, utterly untrue, and monstrous theological and philosophical aberrations and notions.

The glorious word *love* is one of the most abused words in the English language. From being one of the most glorious and divine words in our language, it has become, in the way the large majority of people use it, one of the most weakly and sickly sentimental and really immoral words. Not infrequently, it is a fine-looking cloak for the basest selfishness and vilest lust. Let us turn, then, to the Bible for our definition of what love really means, that is, what God Himself means by love.

Let us look again at 1 John 3:16–17:

By this we know love, because He laid down His life for us. And we also ought to lay down our lives for the brethren. But whoever has this world's goods, and sees his brother in need, and shuts up his heart from him, how does the love of God abide in him?

Here is God's definition, or description, of love: *"By this we know love, because He laid down His life for us."* We see, then, that love is no mere sentimental tenderness, no mere selfish fondness or affection or attraction to another. Love is a self-sacrificing desire for and delight in the welfare of the one loved. You get practically the same definition of love, though phrased in other words, in our Lord's own description of the Father God's love in Matthew 5:44–45:

But I say to you, love your enemies...and pray for those who spitefully use you and persecute you, that you may be sons of your Father in heaven; for He makes His sun rise on the evil and on the good, and sends rain on the just and on the unjust.

WHOM DOES GOD LOVE?

Now another question of fundamental importance confronts us: Whom does God the Father love? Here again we are not left to dream and imagine and speculate for ourselves. God in His own Word tells us in the plainest and most unmistakable language exactly who it is whom He loves.

God Loves His Own Son, Jesus Christ

First, God loves His own Son—His only Son—Jesus Christ our Lord. This truth is set forth again and again in the Bible in the plainest and, at the same time, the most expressive language. Read, for example, Matthew 3:17: *"And suddenly a voice came from heaven, saying, 'This is My beloved Son, in whom I am well pleased.'"* Let me give you a little more literal translation of the original Greek in this passage, a translation that puts more emphasis on the thought that Jesus Christ is the one original and eternal object of God the Father's eternal love: "And behold, a voice out of the heavens saying, 'This is the Son of Me, the Beloved One, in whom I am well pleased.'"

We find God saying the same thing again audibly *"out of the* [luminous] *cloud"* in which He came down at the transfiguration of our Lord, described in Matthew 17:5:

> *While* [Peter] *was still speaking, behold, a bright* [luminous] *cloud overshadowed them; and suddenly a voice came out of the cloud, saying, "This is My beloved Son, in whom I am well pleased. Hear Him!"*

Here again, the Greek, literally translated, would be the same as in Matthew 3:17: "This is the Son of Me, the Beloved One, in whom I am well pleased." We read in Luke 20:13: *"Then the owner of the vineyard said, 'What shall I do? I will send my beloved son. Probably they will respect him when they see him.'"* In this verse, also, the literal Greek meaning of the phrase *"my beloved Son"* is, "the Son of Me, the Beloved One."

Let us look at just one more verse on this particular point, John 17:24:

> *Father, I desire that they also whom You gave Me may be with Me where I am, that they may behold My glory which You have given Me; for You loved Me before the foundation of the world.*

These passages all set forth definitely and clearly the profoundly significant fact that God's own Son, Jesus Christ our Lord, was the original and eternal object of God the Father's love. If God is eternal, and we have already seen that He certainly is, then His love must have an eternal object. There must, therefore, because of a necessity in the Divine Being Himself, be a multiplicity of Persons in the Godhead. The eternal object of the divine love of the Eternal Father is the Eternal Son.

God Loves Those Who Love His Son

Second, God loves those who love His Son—the original and eternal object of His love—and who believe that He, Jesus Christ, came forth from the Father. This fundamentally important truth is set forth in our Lord's own words as they are recorded in John 14:21, 23:

*He who has My commandments and keeps
them, it is he who loves Me. And he who loves
Me will be loved by My Father, and I will love
him and manifest Myself to him....If anyone
loves Me, he will keep My word; and My Father will love him, and We will come to him
and make Our home with him.*

We find that our Lord Jesus taught the same thing
in John 16:27: *"For the Father Himself loves you,
because you have loved Me, and have believed that I
came forth from God."* God loves those who love His
Son and believe that He came forth from the Father,
because of their relationship to His Son, because
they are united to Him by love and faith.

As we will shortly see, God loves all men; but He
has an altogether special love for those who are in
Christ. God has precisely the same love for those
who are in Christ Jesus that He has for Christ Jesus
Himself. Our Lord Himself tells us this in one of the
most astounding statements to be found in the Bible.
You will find it in John 17:23: *"I in them, and You in
Me; that they may be made perfect in one, and that
the world may know that You have sent Me, and have
loved them as You have loved Me."*

Of course, God has a love for people that pre-
cedes their love for Christ. We are distinctly told this
in 1 John 4:19: *"We love Him because He first loved
us."*

God Loves the World

Third, God loves the world, the whole human
race, and each individual member of it. We find this

truth taught in what is perhaps the most familiar verse in the Bible, John 3:16: *"For God so loved the world that He gave His only begotten Son, that whoever believes in Him should not perish but have everlasting life."* The same truth is found in 1 Timothy 2:3–4: *"This is good and acceptable in the sight of God our Savior, who desires all men to be saved and to come to the knowledge of the truth."* This truth is put in still another way in 2 Peter 3:9: *"The Lord is not slack concerning His promise, as some count slackness, but is longsuffering toward us, not willing that any should perish but that all should come to repentance."*

God Loves Sinners

Fourth, God loves the sinner, the ungodly, those dead in sins. This amazing truth is declared again and again in a variety of ways in the Bible. Read these two passages, for example:

> *For when we were still without strength, in due time Christ died for the ungodly. For scarcely for a righteous man will one die; yet perhaps for a good man someone would even dare to die. But God demonstrates His own love toward us, in that while we were still sinners, Christ died for us.* (Rom. 5:6–8)

> *But God, who is rich in mercy, because of His great love with which He loved us, even when we were dead in trespasses, made us alive together with Christ (by grace you have been saved).* (Eph. 2:4–5)

We find this truth in the Old Testament as well as in the New Testament. We find it even in the book of that stern old prophet of the exile, Ezekiel, in Ezekiel 33:11:

> Say to them: "As I live," says the Lord GOD, "I have no pleasure in the death of the wicked, but that the wicked turn from his way and live. Turn, turn from your evil ways! For why should you die, O house of Israel?"

Please note the tender pleading in the words *"Turn, turn."* Of course, God's love for sinners, for the ungodly, for those dead in sins, is included in the meaning of the words *"God so loved the world"*; however, the Bible puts special emphasis upon this fact.

HOW THE LOVE OF GOD MANIFESTS ITSELF

We come now to the very important question, How does the love of God manifest itself? Here we must walk very carefully and be sure that we are going exactly by the Book every step of the way, for it is at just this point that many go astray into all kinds of notions and theological aberrations.

God Ministers to Those He Loves and Protects Them from Evil

In the first place, God's love manifests itself in His ministering to the need and joy of those whom He loves and in His protecting them from all evil. Read Isaiah 48:14, 20–21:

God Is Love

All of you, assemble yourselves, and hear! Who among them has declared these things? The LORD loves him; He shall do His pleasure on Babylon, and His arm shall be against the Chaldeans....Go forth from Babylon! Flee from the Chaldeans! With a voice of singing, declare, proclaim this, utter it to the end of the earth; say, "The LORD has redeemed His servant Jacob!" And they did not thirst when He led them through the deserts; He caused the waters to flow from the rock for them; He also split the rock, and the waters gushed out.

(Isa. 48:14, 20–21)

These are exceedingly beautiful and marvelously comforting words, written before modern philosophy or even ancient Greek philosophy was dreamed of, written more than twenty-five hundred years ago. Who taught Isaiah to write in this way and enabled him to write, so many, many centuries ago, in those exceedingly "dark ages"? There is only one reasonable answer: *God did.* Isaiah "spoke as he was borne along by the Holy Spirit" (see 2 Peter 1:21); his very words were God-breathed. To deny this reality is to be unscientific and irrational, confused and blinded by the narrow-minded and stubborn bigotry of New Theology. Let us ponder deeply the divinely inspired words of Isaiah in the above verses.

But let us go still further back—let us go back nine centuries before Isaiah—to thirty-four hundred years ago. Read Deuteronomy 32:9–12:

For the Lord's portion is His people; Jacob is the place of His inheritance. He found him in a desert land and in the wasteland, a howling wilderness; He encircled him, He instructed

*him, He kept him as the apple of His eye. As
an eagle stirs up its nest, hovers over its
young, spreading out its wings, taking them
up, carrying them on its wings, so the LORD
alone led him, and there was no foreign god
with him.*   *(Deut. 32:9–12)*

Even as mere literature, where could this passage
be matched for sublime imagery and expressive phrasing and masterly metaphor? But it is far more than
mere literature; superlatively fine as it is as literature,
it is the heart-comforting and soul-enthralling truth of
God. It was the truth for those long, long ago ages,
and it is the truth for today. It is truth that we have
not yet outgrown, even for all our boasted intellectual
evolution and progress through these long, long centuries. Yes, it is truth to which we have not yet even
grown up. However, these peerless words are entirely
omitted from an abridged Bible with which I am familiar. The compiler, a professor, unabashedly stated
in the preface to that book, that contemptibly inadequate book, that it singles out and sets in logical order
those parts of the Bible that are of vital interest and
practical value in the present age. You may judge for
yourself whether this claim is true or whether it is an
unabashed, abominable, and ridiculous lie.

Now let us look at a passage found in the very
next chapter of the same wondrous book, which is
found in the Book of Books, Deuteronomy 33:3, 12:

*Yes, He loves the people; all His saints are in
Your hand; they sit down at Your feet; everyone
receives Your words....Of Benjamin he said:
"The beloved of the LORD shall dwell in safety*

by Him, who shelters him all the day long; and
he shall dwell between His shoulders."
                                    (Deut. 33:3, 12)

All this, also, the professor omitted from his book that claims to set forth all those parts of the Bible that are of vital interest and practical value in the present age. Poor, blind man, posing as a thorough Bible scholar and yet so densely ignorant of the full contents of that wondrous Book.

God Chastens His People for Their Benefit

In the second place, God's love manifests itself in His chastening and scourging of His loved ones for their benefit, so that out of this chastening the *"peaceable fruit of righteousness"* may come. We find this taught, for example, in Hebrews 12:5–11:

You have forgotten the exhortation which speaks to you as to sons: "My son, do not despise the chastening of the LORD, nor be discouraged when you are rebuked by Him; for whom the LORD loves He chastens, and scourges every son whom He receives." If you endure chastening, God deals with you as with sons; for what son is there whom a father does not chasten? But if you are without chastening, of which all have become partakers, then you are illegitimate and not sons. Furthermore, we have had human fathers who corrected us, and we paid them respect. Shall we not much more readily be in subjection to the Father of spirits and live? For they indeed for a few days chastened us as seemed best to

them, but He for our profit, that we may be partakers of His holiness. Now no chastening seems to be joyful for the present, but painful; nevertheless, afterward it yields the peaceable fruit of righteousness to those who have been trained by it.
(Heb. 12:5–11)

The fact that God is love and that God loves us is no guarantee that we will never suffer; rather, it is a guarantee that we will suffer, for suffering is just what we sometimes need most. The parent who shelters his child from all suffering, under all circumstances, is not the parent who most truly or most wisely loves his child. No, he loves himself, and he sacrifices his child's highest good to spare his own feelings. But this is not so with our infinitely wise and infinitely loving heavenly Father. He so truly loves us that, although it wounds His own heart, He *"chastens"* and even *"scourges"* us.

Do not falsely comfort yourself with the belief that because God is love and because God loves you with an infinite love, you will never suffer. No, precisely because He does love you, you will surely suffer. And do not think that because you are now undergoing suffering and almost unbearable pain or sorrow, that God does not love you. No, it is because He does love you that you are suffering.

God Himself Is Afflicted in the Afflictions of His People

In the third place, God's love manifests itself in His being Himself afflicted when His loved ones are afflicted, even when their afflictions come from His own hand and are the result of their own sin. This great and comforting fact is set forth in Isaiah 63:9:

In all their affliction He was afflicted, and the Angel of His Presence saved them; in His love and in His pity He redeemed them; and He bore them and carried them all the days of old.

In this verse, God is speaking particularly of the terrible afflictions that overtook the Jewish people. These afflictions were the direct consequence and punishment of their own wrongdoing and came directly or indirectly from God's own hand; they were the result of their own unfaithfulness to God. Yet God tells us that in all these appalling sorrows and calamities, which resulted from their own outrageous sin, the holy God—against whom they had sinned and who sent the suffering upon them—suffered with them. These profound and matchless words were written over twenty-five centuries ago. Who is their real author? Surely not Isaiah, but God. No really intelligent and fair-minded person will attempt to deny it.

Such a Being is the God of the Bible. He is not the cold, abstract, impersonal, emotionless "Absolute" of modern philosophy. He is a Being with a mother's heart, the kind of mother who, although she may see the need for severely punishing her child for his own highest good, nevertheless herself suffers in all that the child suffers. She suffers far more than the child, making all the child's agonies her own; she is pierced to the very heart by them.

Take this truth to heart: There is not an agony or pain or sorrow that any of us suffers, even the keenest anguish that comes from our own most inexcusable wrongdoing, that our Father in heaven does not suffer with us. Let us take in all the wonder and all the comfort of this truth of God that He has set forth in this wonderful Book, this peerless Book, this Book that stands absolutely alone among all the books ever written, a Book clearly proven by the indisputable facts in the case to be the one and only Book that is God-breathed.

God Never Forgets Those Whom He Loves

In the fourth place, God's love is manifested in His never forgetting those whom He loves. We are told this comforting truth in these amazing words found in Isaiah 49:15–16:

> Can a woman forget her nursing child, and not have compassion on the son of her womb? Surely they may forget, yet I will not forget you. See, I have inscribed you on the palms of My hands.

It often seems to us, in our blindness, that God has forgotten us when He, for His own wise reasons, allows sorrows and losses and afflictions of various kinds to accumulate. But He has never forgotten us. A mother may forget her nursing child, but God never forgets—no, not for the smallest moment—those persons who are the objects of His ceaseless and never slumbering love.

God Made the Greatest Sacrifice for Those He Loves

Even now, we have not yet scaled the highest heights or fathomed the deepest depths of the love of the God of the Bible. In the fifth place, God's love has manifested itself by His making the greatest sacrifice in His power for those whom He loves—the sacrifice of His own and only Son to die as the propitiation (or atoning sacrifice) for our sins. Two of the most meaningful statements of this truth are found in 1 John 4:9–10 and John 3:16. Let us first look at 1 John 4:9–10:

> *In this the love of God was manifested toward us, that God has sent His only begotten Son into the world, that we might live through Him. In this is love, not that we loved God, but that He loved us and sent His Son to be the propitiation for our sins.*

Now let us look at John 3:16, which we have all heard so often and know so well, but which we do not know as we should know even yet, and the depths of which we will never fathom until eternity dawns: *"For God so loved the world that He gave His only begotten Son, that whoever believes in Him should not perish but have everlasting life."*

We have seen that love is a self-sacrificing desire for and a delight in the welfare of the one loved; therefore, the true test and measure of love is sacrifice. The sacrifice of Jesus Christ is the measure of God's love for us. If we ever desire to see as far as finite eye can see into the unfathomable depths of the infinite love of God, there is one place to look, and that is to the cross and at the One who hung upon it. We should recall the depth and intensity of the infinite and eternal love of the Father for *"His only begotten Son,"* and then see Him hanging there enduring all the immeasurable agonies of the cross to purchase redemption and eternal life for us. Then, with all this vividly in our minds, we should think of the agonized heart of the Father, who loves His Son with a love immeasurably beyond our comprehension and yet gave Him up—gave Him up not only to die but to die on the cross in our place. This is a matter for us to ponder, to meditate upon; it is not for us to try to put into words, for no words can express all the meaning of it, and all possible illustrations fall infinitely short of describing the reality of it.

God Forgives Sins

In the sixth place, God's love manifests itself in His forgiving sins. The Bible, from Genesis 3 (where sin first entered human history) to Revelation 22, is full of this truth. Let us look at one passage from among the many that might be cited:

> *Indeed it was for my own peace that I had great bitterness; but You have lovingly delivered my soul from the pit of corruption, for You have cast all my sins behind Your back.*
>
> *(Isa. 38:17)*

God, because of His love for us, will forgive the sins of any sinner, no matter how many and how great his sins may be, if he, on his part, will turn away from his sins and turn to God. Listen to the way in which it is put in Isaiah 55:7:

> *Let the wicked forsake his way, and the unrighteous man his thoughts; let him return to the LORD, and He will have mercy on him; and*

to our God, for He will abundantly pardon.
                                              (Isa. 55:7)

Of course, God will not forgive our sins if we will not forsake them. To do that would not be love. But God will forgive them, one and all, will utterly blot them out, no matter how many and how black they may be, if we will turn from them.

God Gives Us Life, Raises Us with Christ, Seats Us in Heavenly Places, Shows Us the Riches of His Grace

In the seventh place, God's love manifests itself in His (1) imparting life to those who are *"dead in trespasses"* and sins, (2) raising them up together with Christ, (3) making them to *"sit together"* with Christ *"in the heavenly places,"* and (4) showing to us in the *"ages to come...the exceeding riches of His grace in His kindness toward us in Christ Jesus."* In this section, I have combined four manifestations of God's love because God Himself groups them together in Ephesians 2:4–7:

> *God, who is rich in mercy, because of His great love with which He loved us, even when we were dead in trespasses, made us alive together with Christ (by grace you have been saved), and raised us up together, and made us sit together in the heavenly places in Christ Jesus, that in the ages to come He might show the exceeding riches of His grace in His kindness toward us in Christ Jesus.*

Any one of these four manifestations of God's love is worthy of prolonged contemplation and meditation. But let us also consider that, even now, notwithstanding all the wonders God's love has worked,

God has only begun doing works of love for us. The fullness of God's love has not yet been manifested. It has just begun to unfold itself. As John put it in 1 John 3:2, *"Beloved, now we are children of God; and it has not yet been revealed what we shall be."* It is *"in the ages to come"* that God will *"show the exceeding riches of His grace in His kindness toward us in Christ Jesus."*

God Makes Us His Children

In the eighth place, God's love manifests itself in His granting to us that we may be called the *"children of God."* This we find declared in God's Word in 1 John 3:1: *"Behold what manner of love the Father hath bestowed upon us, that we should be called children of God; and such we are"* (ASV).

When we stop to think about what sort of a Being God Himself is, even as we have so imperfectly come to understand Him in the preceding chapters of this book, and when we stop to think of what sort of beings we ourselves are, this is one of the most amazing manifestations of the love of God. Would it not be amazing if the wisest, noblest, richest, and most powerful monarch of earth rode down to the slums of some city of his realm and, seeing a filthy, ragged, dirty, ignorant, miserable, and degenerate child standing by the side of the road, stopped and said to this disreputable, outcast lad, "Come, get in here with me. I will take you to the royal palace and adopt you into my family; you will bear my name and be my heir"? Yes, that would be marvelous, incredibly marvelous. However, it would not be one millionth as amazing as the fact that the great, eternal, omnipotent, omniscient, infinitely holy God

184

came down to the vile slums of this fallen and corrupt earth of ours and picked you and me out in our ignorance, folly, weakness, poverty, moral vileness, and depravity, and said, "I will adopt you into My family and give you the right to be called My children." Read it again from God's own Word: *"Behold what manner of love the Father hath bestowed upon us, that we should be called children of God; and such we are"* (1 John 3:1 ASV). Why would God make us His children? It is because of God's love, because *"God is love"* (1 John 4:8, 16).

God Rejoices over His People and Rests in His Love

In the ninth place, God's love manifests itself in His rejoicing over His saved people with joy and singing, and resting in His love for them. Here again, we turn to an utterance of long, long ago, about twenty-five hundred fifty years ago, about six hundred twenty-five years before our Lord Jesus was born in Bethlehem. You will find it in Zephaniah 3:17:

> *Jehovah thy God is in the midst of thee, a mighty one who will save; he will rejoice over thee with joy; he will rest in his love; he will joy over thee with singing.*   *(ASV)*

What a marvelous and heart-stirring picture we have here! In this passage, we see the infinite God, the Creator and Upholder not only of the whole earth but of the sun, moon, and stars—those vast worlds of light in all their countless numbers and inconceivably vast magnitude—taking such a tender interest in beings as insignificant and morally worthless as we are, that, when we are saved, He rejoices over us as a mother croons over the child who nestles to her bosom, singing a sweet lullaby as He draws us to His heart and rests in His love. The Hebrew word translated *"rest"* in this verse is a deeply significant word. Literally translated, the passage would read, "He will be silent in His love." That is, His love is perfectly satisfied, and He rests in a rapturous silence that is deeper than any words can express. Oh, such is God, such is the God of the Bible! He is not the god of Christian Science, New Thought, Theosophy, Spiritualism, modern philosophy, or New Theology. He is the God of the one and only really wonderful Book, the Book that is unmistakably His own Book, the Bible.

Chapter 10

GOD IS RIGHTEOUS

The LORD is righteous in all His ways.
—Psalm 145:17

A s we begin to consider this fundamentally important subject of the righteousness of God, I would like to call your attention to some specific passages of Scripture that will form the basis of our study. Many Scripture texts suggest themselves to us when we think of this aspect of the character of God, for both the Old and New Testaments are full of the great theme of God's righteousness. Let us begin with some passages from the Old Testament:

> *O LORD God of Israel, You are righteous, for we are left as a remnant, as it is this day. Here we are before You, in our guilt, though no one can stand before You because of this!*
> *(Ezra 9:15)*

> *You are the LORD God, who chose Abram, and brought him out of Ur of the Chaldeans, and gave him the name Abraham; You found his*

heart faithful before You, and made a covenant with him to give the land of the Canaanites, the Hittites, the Amorites, the Perizzites, the Jebusites, and the Girgashites; to give it to his descendants. You have performed Your words, for You are righteous. (Neh. 9:7–8)

I will extol You, my God, O King....I will meditate on the glorious splendor of Your majesty, and on Your wondrous works....The LORD upholds all who fall, and raises up all who are bowed down. The eyes of all look expectantly to You, and You give them their food in due season. You open Your hand and satisfy the desire of every living thing. The LORD is righteous in all His ways, gracious in all His works. The LORD is near to all who call upon Him, to all who call upon Him in truth. He will fulfill the desire of those who fear Him; He also will hear their cry and save them. (Ps. 145:1, 5, 14–19)

And He [the Lord] has confirmed His words, which He spoke against us and against our judges who judged us, by bringing upon us a great disaster; for under the whole heaven such has never been done as what has been done to Jerusalem. As it is written in the Law of Moses, all this disaster has come upon us; yet we have not made our prayer before the LORD our God, that we might turn from our iniquities and understand Your truth. Therefore the LORD has kept the disaster in mind, and brought it upon us; for the LORD our God is righteous in all the works which He does,

though we have not obeyed His voice.
(Dan. 9:12–14)

Oh, sing to the LORD a new song! For He has done marvelous things; His right hand and His holy arm have gained Him the victory. The LORD has made known His salvation; His righteousness He has revealed in the sight of the nations. He has remembered His mercy and His faithfulness to the house of Israel; all the ends of the earth have seen the salvation of our God. *(Ps. 98:1–3)*

Let the heavens rejoice, and let the earth be glad; let the sea roar, and all its fullness; let the field be joyful, and all that is in it. Then all the trees of the woods will rejoice before the LORD. For He is coming, for He is coming to judge the earth. He shall judge the world with righteousness, and the peoples with His truth. *(Ps. 96:11–13)*

Let us now turn to the New Testament, starting with the words of our Lord Jesus Christ Himself:

O righteous Father! The world has not known You, but I have known You; and these have known that You sent Me. *(John 17:25)*

Next, let us look at one of the most important passages on this subject to be found in the entire Bible:

But now the righteousness of God apart from the law is revealed, being witnessed by the Law and the Prophets, even the righteousness of God, through faith in Jesus Christ, to all and on all who believe. For there is no difference; for all have sinned and fall short of the glory of God, being justified freely by His grace through the redemption that is in Christ Jesus, whom God set forth as a propitiation by His blood, through faith; to demonstrate His righteousness, because in His forbearance God had passed over the sins that were previously committed, to demonstrate at the present time His righteousness, that He might be just and the justifier of the one who has faith in Jesus.

(Rom. 3:21–26)

The Greek word rendered *"just"* in the last verse of this passage is precisely the same word that is elsewhere rendered *"righteous."* It is rendered *"just"* in this passage to show that it is from the same root as the word *"justifier,"* which comes three words later.

Now let us read 1 John 1:9:

If we confess our sins, He is faithful and just [righteous] to forgive us our sins and to cleanse us from all unrighteousness.

The final three texts are all from the last book in the Bible, a book whose whole theme is the righteousness of God:

And I saw something like a sea of glass mingled with fire, and those who have the victory over the beast, over his image and over his

*mark and over the number of his name, stand-
ing on the sea of glass, having harps of God.
They sing the song of Moses, the servant of
God, and the song of the Lamb, saying: "Great
and marvelous are Your works, Lord God Almighty! Just* [righteous] *and true are Your
ways, O King of the saints! Who shall not fear
You, O Lord, and glorify Your name? For You
alone are holy. For all nations shall come and
worship before You, for Your judgments
[*"righteous acts,"* ASV] *have been manifested."*
(Rev. 15:2–4)*

*Then the third angel poured out his bowl on
the rivers and springs of water, and they became blood. And I heard the angel of the waters saying: "You are righteous, O Lord, the
One who is and who was and who is to be, because You have judged these things. For they
have shed the blood of saints and prophets,
and You have given them blood to drink. For it
is their just due." And I heard another from
the altar saying, "Even so, Lord God Almighty, true and righteous are Your judgments."* (Rev. 16:4–7)

*After these things I heard a loud voice of a
great multitude in heaven, saying, "Alleluia!
Salvation and glory and honor and power be-
long to the Lord our God! For true and righteous are His judgments."* (Rev. 19:1–2)

THE LORD GOD IS RIGHTEOUS

In our first and second texts, in others that we
have just read, and in still others that I did not have
room to include, we are told in so many words that

191

Jehovah, the God of the Bible, the God of both the Old Testament and the New Testament, is righteous. In our third text, we read that *"the LORD is righteous in all His ways"* (Ps. 145:17), and our fourth text says that *"the LORD our God is righteous in all the works which He does"* (Dan. 9:14). Heaven and earth, men and angels, inspired lawgivers, prophets, psalmists, apostles, and our Lord Jesus Himself, join together in these passages in one great and triumphant "Hallelujah Chorus" that Jehovah, our God Almighty, the God of the Bible, is a righteous God.

WHAT DOES "RIGHTEOUS" MEAN?

We come now to the all-important question, What does the word *righteous* mean as it is used in the Bible? We go, of course, to the Bible itself for an answer to this question. The only definitions of biblical terms that are of any real value are biblical definitions. And the Bible defines, in a very clear, very definite, and very explicit way, just what *righteous* means.

Our first definition is in Ezekiel 18:5: *"But if a man is just and does what is lawful and right...."* In this verse, the word *"just"* is used instead of *righteous*. (See also KJV, ASV, and RV.) However, as in the passage from Romans 3 that we looked at earlier (but in relation to the Greek language), the word for *"just"* here is the same word in Hebrew that is elsewhere translated *"righteous."* Let me mention that all the way through the Old Testament (in the NKJV, KJV, ASV, and RV), the same Hebrew word is sometimes translated *"righteous"* and sometimes *"just."* In addition, all the way through the New Testament (in the same Bible versions), the same Greek word is sometimes translated *"righteous"* and sometimes *"just."* "Righteousness" and "justice" are not two different attributes of God; the two words are used for precisely the same thing. *Righteous* is the preferable word, as it conforms more closely to the exact derivation of the word.

But to go back to the definition of *"just"* or "righteous" in Ezekiel 18:5, we see that to be righteous is to have the kind of character that leads one to always do *"what is lawful and right."* We find practically the same definition of *"righteous,"* but partly in a negative form, in Zephaniah 3:5: *"The Lord is righteous in her midst, He will do no unrighteousness. Every morning He brings His justice to light; He never fails."*

The Hebrew word in the Old Testament sometimes translated *"righteous"* and sometimes *"just,"* means "right" or "straight," according to its etymology, or word origin. The etymology of our English word *"righteous" is* precisely the same. The Greek word in the New Testament sometimes translated *"righteous"* and sometimes *"just"* means, according to its etymology, "that which is conformed to custom or usage." However, the Greek word, as used in the New Testament, derives its significance from its being used in the Greek translation of the Old Testament that was in common use in our Lord's day and in the days of the apostles, called the Septuagint. This word was used in the Septuagint to translate the Hebrew word meaning "right" or "straight." Therefore, the righteousness, or justice, of the God of the Bible is the attribute of God that leads Him always, and under all circumstances, to do what is "right" or "straight."

The meaning of the "righteousness" of God is not to be limited, as is so often done in modern theological usage, to God's punitive justice. God's punitive justice is, as we will shortly see, only one manifestation of the justice, or righteousness, of God; it is not the manifestation of God's righteousness that is most prominent in the biblical usage of the word.

Moreover, God's righteousness is closely related to His holiness, but they are not exactly the same. Holiness seems to refer more to God's character as He is in Himself. Righteousness seems to refer more to His character as it is manifested in His dealings with others.

HOW THE RIGHTEOUSNESS OF GOD MANIFESTS ITSELF

This brings us directly to the question, and it is a tremendously important question, How does the righteousness of God manifest itself? Here again, we must walk very carefully and go by the Book itself every step of the way. There are many preachers, theologians, and dreamers of many kinds who do not go by the Book but chase the iridescent yet unsubstantial bubbles blown by their own brilliant fancies, and they wind up in no-man's-land. But let us turn to the Book of God, and then we will get somewhere. Indeed, we will find ourselves in a fine and fair country, lying down in *"green pastures"* and walking beside *"still waters"* (Ps. 23:2).

God Loves Righteousness and Hates Iniquity

First, the righteousness of God manifests itself in His loving righteousness and hating iniquity. Read Psalm 11:4–7:

God Is Righteous

The LORD is in His holy temple, the Lord's throne is in heaven; His eyes behold, His eyelids test the sons of men. The LORD tests the righteous, but the wicked and the one who loves violence His soul hates. Upon the wicked He will rain coals; fire and brimstone and a burning wind shall be the portion of their cup. For the LORD is righteous, He loves righteousness; His countenance beholds the upright.

(Ps. 11:4–7)

God is infinitely righteous; therefore, He loves righteousness with an infinite love and hates iniquity, in all its forms, with an infinite hatred.

It is thought by some that since God is love, there can be no such thing as hatred of any kind in God. Yet it is precisely because God is love, infinite love, that He hates with infinite hatred all that harms those whom He loves. He hates sin with infinite hatred because He loves the sinner with infinite love. I hate tuberculosis with intense hatred because I love my daughter, upon whom the foul thing has fastened itself. The righteous God not only loves righteousness with infinite love, but He also hates all iniquity with infinite hatred, both because He is righteous and because He is love. The righteous God of the Bible's hatred of sin is as intense as His love of righteousness. This sweet, sentimental, sickish, silly, rationalizing talk about sin that is so common today among a certain type of would-be social philosophers and ethical teachers arises from a sad lack in their moral makeup, a lack of real and Godlike righteousness; they are moral anemics. A really righteous person, a person of Godlike righteousness, hates sin as truly and as intensely as he loves righteousness.

God Carries Out upon Sinners Their Due Punishment

Second, the righteousness of God manifests itself in His carrying out upon sinners the punishment due for their sins. This great fact, which we would do well to always bear in mind, comes out again and again in the Word of God. For example, read Exodus 9:23–27:

> *And Moses stretched out his rod toward heaven; and the LORD sent thunder and hail, and fire darted to the ground. And the LORD rained hail on the land of Egypt. So there was hail, and fire mingled with the hail, so very heavy that there was none like it in all the land of Egypt since it became a nation. And the hail struck throughout the whole land of Egypt, all that was in the field, both man and beast; and the hail struck every herb of the field and broke every tree of the field. Only in the land of Goshen, where the children of Israel were, there was no hail. And Pharaoh sent and called for Moses and Aaron, and said to them, "I have sinned this time. The LORD is righteous, and my people and I are wicked."*

The same important truth is found in 2 Chronicles 12:5–6:

> *Then Shemaiah the prophet came to Rehoboam and the leaders of Judah, who were gathered together in Jerusalem because of Shishak, and said to them, "Thus says the LORD: 'You have forsaken Me, and therefore I also have left you in the hand of Shishak.'" So*

the leaders of Israel and the king humbled themselves; and they said, "The LORD is righteous." *(2 Chron. 12:5–6)*

Daniel proclaimed the same truth in Daniel 9:12–14:

He has confirmed His words, which He spoke against us and against our judges who judged us, by bringing upon us a great disaster; for under the whole heaven such has never been done as what has been done to Jerusalem. As it is written in the Law of Moses, all this disaster has come upon us; yet we have not made our prayer before the LORD our God, that we might turn from our iniquities and understand Your truth. Therefore the LORD has kept the disaster in mind, and brought it upon us; for the LORD our God is righteous in all the works which He does, though we have not obeyed His voice.

We also find it set forth in a most vivid and impressive way in the last book of the Bible, in Revelation 16:5–6:

And I heard the angel of the waters saying: "You are righteous, O Lord, the One who is and who was and who is to be, because You have judged these things. For they have shed the blood of saints and prophets, and You have given them blood to drink. For it is their just due."

Since God is righteous, we may put it down as absolutely certain that, if we sin, we must suffer, and suffer for every sin we commit. This universe in which we live is governed at all times and under all circumstances by a God who is absolutely, unwaveringly, and unceasingly righteous. So it is certain that if we commit any wrong act, great or small, we are bound to be the losers for it. In every instance, a righteous God must and will inflict upon every unrepentant sinner the punishment due for his sin.

God Bestows upon the Righteous Their Due Reward

Third, the righteousness of God manifests itself in His bestowing upon the righteous the reward due for their faithfulness. We are told this over and over again in God's own revelation of Himself, the Bible, in a variety of ways but with one meaning. For example, we read in 2 Timothy 4:8:

> *Finally, there is laid up for me the crown of righteousness, which the Lord, the righteous Judge, will give to me on that Day, and not to me only but also to all who have loved His appearing.*

Turning back to the Old Testament, we read in 1 Kings 8:32:

> *Then hear in heaven, and act, and judge Your servants, condemning the wicked, bringing his way on his head, and justifying the righteous by giving him according to his righteousness.*

And the psalmist sang in Psalm 7:9–11,

> *Oh, let the wickedness of the wicked come to an end, but establish the just* [righteous]; *for the*

righteous God tests the hearts and minds. My defense is of God, who saves the upright in heart. God is a just [righteous] judge, and God is angry with the wicked every day.
(Ps. 7:9–11)

We may be sure that if we sin, we will suffer. However, because God is a righteous God, we may be equally sure that if we do any righteous act, great or small, we will not miss our full reward. As our Lord Jesus put it in Matthew 10:42,

And whoever gives one of these little ones only a cup of cold water in the name of a disciple, assuredly, I say to you, he shall by no means lose his reward.

God Protects and Delivers His People

Fourth, the righteousness of God is manifested in His protecting and delivering His people from all their adversaries. The book of Psalms is especially rich in the setting forth of this precious truth:

Oh, sing to the LORD a new song! For He has done marvelous things; His right hand and His holy arm have gained Him the victory. The LORD has made known His salvation; His righteousness He has revealed in the sight of the nations. He has remembered His mercy and His faithfulness to the house of Israel; all the ends of the earth have seen the salvation of our God. *(Ps. 98:1–3)*

The LORD executes righteousness and justice for all who are oppressed. *(Ps. 103:6)*

"Many a time they have afflicted me from my youth," let Israel now say; "many a time they have afflicted me from my youth; yet they have not prevailed against me. The plowers plowed on my back; they made their furrows long." The LORD is righteous; He has cut in pieces the cords of the wicked. (Ps. 129:1–4)

Turning now to the New Testament, we read in 2 Thessalonians 1:6–8:

It is a righteous thing with God to repay with tribulation those who trouble you, and to give you who are troubled rest with us when the Lord Jesus is revealed from heaven with His mighty angels, in flaming fire.

In modern theological discussions, we hear more of the justice, or righteousness, of God in relation to the punishment of sinners; but in the Bible, we read more of it in relation to the protection of His people. In modern usage, the righteousness of God is more frequently held up as an attribute of God at which sinners should tremble; but in the Bible, it is constantly dwelt upon as an attribute of God in which His people should rejoice and be confident. We see this, for example, in Psalm 96:11–13:

Let the heavens rejoice, and let the earth be glad; let the sea roar, and all its fullness; let the field be joyful, and all that is in it. Then all the trees of the woods will rejoice before the LORD. For He is coming, for He is coming to judge the earth. He shall judge the world with righteousness, and the peoples with His truth.

God Is Righteous

The prophet Jeremiah, even though he is often called "the weeping prophet," sang the same song of optimistic confidence in the righteous God who protects and delivers His faithful people from all their adversaries and oppressors. We read in Jeremiah 9:24:

> *"But let him who glories glory in this, that he understands and knows Me, that I am the LORD, exercising lovingkindness, judgment, and righteousness in the earth. For in these I delight," says the LORD.*

Let us return to the Psalms again, and read this passage:

> *Gracious is the LORD, and righteous; yes, our God is merciful. The LORD preserves the simple; I was brought low, and He saved me.*
>
> *(Ps. 116:5–6)*

Again, the sweet singer of Israel chanted the same theme of triumphant praise for a righteous God in Psalm 145:15–19:

> *The eyes of all look expectantly to You, and You give them their food in due season. You open Your hand and satisfy the desire of every living thing. The LORD is righteous in all His ways, gracious in all His works. The LORD is near to all who call upon Him, to all who call upon Him in truth. He will fulfill the desire of those who fear Him; He also will hear their cry and save them.*

And the song both of Moses, the stern lawgiver, and of the Lamb, the gracious Savior, as described in the last book in the Bible, has the same jubilant confidence in a righteous God. We read in Revelation 15:3:

> They sing the song of Moses, the servant of God, and the song of the Lamb, saying: "Great and marvelous are Your works, Lord God Almighty! Just [righteous] and true are Your ways, O King of the saints!"

Even the righteousness of God in the punishment of the sinner is frequently spoken of in its relation to and connection with the deliverance and avenging of His people. Let us look at two passages that illustrate this point:

> We ourselves boast of you among the churches of God for your patience and faith in all your persecutions and tribulations that you endure, which is manifest evidence of the righteous judgment of God, that you may be counted worthy of the kingdom of God, for which you also suffer; since it is a righteous thing with God to repay with tribulation those who trouble you, and to give you who are troubled rest with us when the Lord Jesus is revealed from heaven with His mighty angels.
>
> (2 Thess. 1:4–7)

> After these things I heard a loud voice of a great multitude in heaven, saying, "Alleluia! Salvation and glory and honor and power belong to

*the Lord our God! For true and righteous are
His judgments, because He has judged the great
harlot who corrupted the earth with her fornica-
tion; and He has avenged on her the blood of
His servants shed by her."*   *(Rev. 19:1–2)*

Now let us look at another passage from the last
book in the Bible, whose theme is, to a large extent,
the righteousness of God:

*Then the third angel poured out his bowl on
the rivers and springs of water, and they became blood. And I heard the angel of the waters saying: "You are righteous, O Lord, the
One who is and who was and who is to be, because You have judged these things. For they
have shed the blood of saints and prophets,
and You have given them blood to drink. For it
is their just due." And I heard another from
the altar saying, "Even so, Lord God Almighty, true and righteous are Your judgments."*   *(Rev. 16:4–7)*

Here it is the vindication and the avenging of His
people, rather than the suffering of the wicked, that
is the prominent thought.

God Always Keeps His Promises

Fifth, the righteousness of God is manifested in
God's always keeping His promises to the very letter. The Levites in Nehemiah's day saw this and declared it twenty-three hundred years ago. They sang
to Jehovah in Nehemiah 9:7–8,

> *You are the LORD God, who chose Abram, and*
> *brought him out of Ur of the Chaldeans, and*
> *gave him the name Abraham; You found his*
> *heart faithful before You, and made a covenant*
> *with him to give the land of the Canaanites,*
> *the Hittites, the Amorites, the Perizzites, the*
> *Jebusites, and the Girgashites; to give it to his*
> *descendants. You have performed Your words,*
> *for You are righteous.* (Neh. 9:7–8)

Every promise of God is absolutely sure, for He is a righteous God; therefore, He will keep His every word and fulfill His every promise to the last letter.

> How firm a foundation, ye saints of the Lord,
> Is laid for your faith in His excellent Word!

Why is this so? It is because God is righteous; therefore, He will not, and He cannot, lie.

God Provided an Atoning Sacrifice and Justifies Those Who Have Faith in Christ

Sixth, the righteousness of God is manifested in His providing a propitiation, or atoning sacrifice, through which sin was forgiven, and in His justifying the person who has faith in the Substitute, the Savior, who made the propitiation. We read in Romans 3:25–26:

> *God set forth* [Jesus Christ] *as a propitiation by*
> *His blood, through faith, to demonstrate His*
> *righteousness, because in His forbearance God*
> *had passed over the sins that were previously*

committed, to demonstrate at the present time
His righteousness, that He might be just and
the justifier of the one who has faith in Jesus.
(Rom. 3:25–26)

God is a righteous God and consequently must punish sin, for that is the *right* thing to do. Therefore, if the sinner himself is to be forgiven, the punishment for his sins must fall somewhere else; it must fall upon a lawful substitute. There is only one Person in all the universe upon whom the punishment could justly fall and who, at the same time, could be a sufficient sacrifice—the only One who is at the same time both God and Man, Jesus Christ our Lord.

We saw in chapter 8, "God Is Holy," that the atonement made by the death of Jesus Christ found its first demand in the infinite holiness of the only true God, the God of the Bible; but it also found its demand in the infinite righteousness of God. A righteous God must punish sin because that is the right thing to do. Therefore, if you and I were to be spared, Jesus Christ had to bear the penalty in our place. This truth was beautifully brought out twenty-six hundred years ago in those "very dark and unenlightened ages" when our wonderful modern universities were not even dreamed of: *"All we like sheep have gone astray; we have turned, every one, to his own way; and the LORD has laid on Him the iniquity of us all"* (Isa. 53:6).

But that is not all. Since Christ Jesus has borne the penalty of the sins of all who put their confidence in Him as their Substitute, their Savior, then God, because He is righteous, must justify everyone who has faith in Jesus. So, in the atoning death of His Son, who was God manifested in the flesh, God is seen as both just (righteous) and the Justifier (the One who declares righteous) of everyone who believes in Jesus. (See Romans 3:26.) Oh, how glad I am that the God of the Bible, the only true God, is righteous. That fact makes me positively sure that God has absolutely nothing in His account books against me; for Jesus Christ settled my account, and a righteous God will not ask that the same account be settled twice. Are you taking this in?

God Forgives Our Sins When We Confess Them

Finally, the righteousness of God is manifested in the immediate forgiveness of the sins of every believer in Jesus Christ when he confesses his sins to God. John stated this definitely, clearly, beautifully, and forcefully in 1 John, which was perhaps the last book to be written of all the sixty-six books that make up the Bible. Read 1 John 1:9: *"If we confess our sins, he is faithful and righteous to forgive us our sins, and to cleanse us from all unrighteousness"* (ASV). The King James Version translates this as, *"He is faithful and just,"* but the word translated *"just"* in this verse is precisely the same word that is elsewhere translated *"righteous,"* and it should be translated in that way here also.

Therefore, not only the faithfulness of God but the righteousness of God is pledged for the forgiveness of every sin of the believer the moment he confesses it to God. Many Christians wander in darkness and gloom for days because, in a moment of weakness, they have permitted some sin to come into their lives.

That is entirely unnecessary. The moment we discover that we have sinned, we should hurry away to God (not away *from* God but *to* God) and fully, freely, and frankly confess our sin to Him, without any attempt at self-justification or rationalization for our wickedness. Then we can know that God has put away that sin forever. And then—praise God!—there will not be the smallest cloud between us and God, for fellowship will be completely restored just as if we had never sinned. God is righteous and has pledged Himself, His Word, and the atoning blood of Jesus Christ to forgive every one of our sins the moment they are confessed to Him. Thus we can walk in the cloudless sunshine of fellowship with the God of the Bible every day and every hour, no matter how weak we may be or no matter how sad our fall may have been.

> And He walks with me,
> And He talks with me,
> And He tells me that I am His friend.

Oh, let us read the promise once more from the sure Word of God: *"If we confess our sins, he is faithful and righteous to forgive us our sins, and to cleanse us from all unrighteousness"* (1 John 1:9 ASV).

Chapter 11

GOD IS ABUNDANT IN LOVINGKINDNESS

The lovingkindness of Jehovah is from
everlasting to everlasting upon them that fear him.
—Psalm 103:17 ASV

To begin our study of the lovingkindness, or mercy, of God, let us read a collection of passages from the Word of God that will be the foundation stones, tried and true, upon which the whole superstructure of this chapter will be erected. These may seem like a large number of texts. However, as I searched and pondered the Scriptures on this subject (which the Word of God abounds in) it was difficult to reduce them even to these. I know that it won't be tedious but rather the most attention-keeping, delightful, and thrilling part of the entire chapter. In the rest of the chapter, I will aim only to interpret their teaching on the great theme that we have before us.

We may group together the teachings found in these verses and others that I will introduce later—if we are to treat the subject with anything like adequate fullness—under three general headings:

1. God is Full of Lovingkindness
2. To Whom the Lovingkindness of God is Manifested
3. How the Lovingkindness of God is Manifested

However, before we read the verses and look at these three aspects of our discussion, let me ask you to pay very close attention to the fact that, in English versions of the Old Testament, the same Hebrew word is sometimes translated *"mercy"* and sometimes *"lovingkindness."* These two words, therefore, in the usage of the Old Testament, mean precisely the same thing. This Hebrew word should have been translated uniformly either one way or the other. To complicate things a little more, the word *"mercy"* in our English translations of the Old Testament is, in a few instances, a translation of a different Hebrew word. This latter Hebrew word corresponds to the Greek word that is always translated "compassion" in the New Testament. It covers essentially the same idea as *compassion*.

What we need to keep in mind for our study is that the primary meaning of the Hebrew word most frequently used is "kindness," especially kindness exercised toward the suffering or sinning. When this Hebrew word is used, the American Standard Edition of the Revised Version, for the most part, varies from other versions of the Bible and translates it as *"lovingkindness"* and not *"mercy."* This is, on the whole, a better translation of the Hebrew word. Therefore, we will use it uniformly to translate this Hebrew word and will confine the use of the word *mercy* to the translation of the other Hebrew word, the word that corresponds to the Greek word that is translated "compassion" in the New Testament. In keeping with this preference, many of the verses listed in this chapter are given in the American Standard Edition of the Revised Version. You will notice the variety of passages from different books in both the Old and New Testaments—written hundreds or thousands of years apart—that establish the fact that the Lord is abounding in lovingkindness. Let us absorb this great thought into our hearts and minds as we read the following texts. We will begin with three passages from the Psalms:

> *Jehovah is merciful and gracious, slow to anger, and abundant in lovingkindness.*
> *(Ps. 103:8 ASV)*

> *Also unto thee, O Lord, belongeth lovingkindness; for thou renderest to every man according to his work.* *(Ps. 62:12 ASV)*

> *Jehovah is gracious, and merciful; slow to anger, and of great lovingkindness.*
> *(Ps. 145:8 ASV)*

Now let us look at a passage from one of the oldest books in the Bible:

> *(For the LORD your God is a merciful God), He will not forsake you nor destroy you, nor forget the covenant of your fathers which He swore to them.* *(Deut. 4:31)*

Our next text is a New Testament Scripture from the writings of the apostle Paul. He quoted from the Old Testament and then made an additional comment:

> For He says to Moses, "I will have mercy on whomever I will have mercy, and I will have compassion on whomever I will have compassion."...Therefore He has mercy on whom He wills, and whom He wills He hardens.
>
> (Rom. 9:15, 18)

Let us again read several passages from the Old Testament:

> Know therefore that Jehovah thy God, he is God, the faithful God, who keepeth covenant and lovingkindness with them that love him and keep his commandments to a thousand generations. (Deut. 7:9 ASV)

> Thou shalt not bow down thyself unto them, nor serve them [idols]; for I Jehovah thy God am a jealous God, visiting the iniquity of the fathers upon the children, upon the third and upon the fourth generation of them that hate me, and showing lovingkindness unto thousands ["a thousand generations," ASV, margin], of them that love me and keep my commandments. (Exod. 20:5–6 ASV)

> For as the heavens are high above the earth, so great is his lovingkindness toward them that fear him....But the lovingkindness of Jehovah

is from everlasting to everlasting upon them that fear him, and his righteousness unto children's children. (Ps. 103:11, 17 ASV)

Now let us turn to one of the historical books of the Old Testament:

And [Solomon] said, O Jehovah, the God of Israel, there is no God like thee, in heaven, or on earth; who keepest covenant and lovingkindness with thy servants, that walk before thee with all their heart. (2 Chron. 6:14 ASV)

Next are several passages from Proverbs and the Psalms:

He who covers his sins will not prosper, but whoever confesses and forsakes them will have mercy. (Prov. 28:13)

Many sorrows shall be to the wicked; but he that trusteth in Jehovah, lovingkindness shall compass him about. (Ps. 32:10 ASV)

For thou, Lord, art good, and ready to forgive, and abundant in lovingkindness unto all them that call upon thee. (Ps. 86:5 ASV)

Let us now look at a passage from the book of Numbers, which records the wanderings of the Israelites in the desert for forty years after being delivered from slavery in Egypt.

[Moses said to the Lord,] Thou hast spoken, saying, Jehovah is slow to anger, and abundant in lovingkindness, forgiving iniquity and

213

*transgression; and that will by no means clear
the guilty, visiting the iniquity of the fathers
upon the children, upon the third and upon the
fourth generation. Pardon, I pray thee, the iniquity of this people according unto the greatness of thy lovingkindness, and according as
thou hast forgiven this people, from Egypt even
until now. And Jehovah said, I have pardoned
according to thy word.* (Num. 14:17–20 ASV)

Next, we will hear from two of the prophets:

*Let the wicked forsake his way, and the un-
righteous man his thoughts; let him return to
the LORD, and He will have mercy on him; and
to our God, for He will abundantly pardon.*
                                    (Isa. 55:7)

*Who is a God like unto thee, that pardoneth
iniquity, and passeth over the transgression of
the remnant of his heritage? he retaineth not
his anger for ever, because he delighteth in lovingkindness.* (Mic. 7:18 ASV)

We go now to one of the last books to be written
in the Old Testament:

[The Levites and others prayed,] *"But* [the Israelites in the time of Moses] *and our fathers
acted proudly, hardened their necks, and did
not heed Your commandments. They refused to
obey, and they were not mindful of Your wonders that You did among them. But they hardened their necks, and in their rebellion they
appointed a leader to return to their bondage.*

214

But You are God, ready to pardon, gracious and merciful, slow to anger, abundant in kindness, and did not forsake them....Nevertheless they were disobedient and rebelled against You, cast Your law behind their backs and killed Your prophets, who testified against them to turn them to Yourself; and they worked great provocations. Therefore You delivered them into the hand of their enemies, who oppressed them; and in the time of their trouble, when they cried to You, You heard from heaven; and according to Your abundant mercies You gave them deliverers who saved them from the hand of their enemies....Yet for many years You had patience with them, and testified against them by Your Spirit in Your prophets. Yet they would not listen; therefore You gave them into the hand of the peoples of the lands. Nevertheless in Your great mercy You did not utterly consume them nor forsake them; for You are God, gracious and merciful." (Neh. 9:16–17, 26–27, 30–31)

Now let us read one of Paul's New Testament epistles:

For indeed he [Paul's fellow worker Epaphroditus] *was sick almost unto death; but God had mercy on him, and not only on him but on me also, lest I should have sorrow upon sorrow.* (Phil. 2:27)

Finally, let us look at two verses from the Old Testament:

Thou in thy lovingkindness hast led the people that thou hast redeemed: thou hast guided them

in thy strength to thy holy habitation.
(Exod. 15:13 ASV)

But I will sing of thy strength; yea, I will sing
aloud of thy lovingkindness in the morning:
for thou hast been my high tower, and a refuge
in the day of my distress. *(Ps. 59:16 ASV)*

GOD IS FULL OF LOVINGKINDNESS

In our first four texts, we are told that the Lord
Jehovah, the God of the Bible, is full of mercy, that
He is abundant in lovingkindness. All these passages
are from the Old Testament, which is supposed, by
some of our modern, so-called advanced scholars, to
present a stern, severe, and relentless God, in contrast to the gentle and loving Father of whom Jesus
and John spoke. In one of the later texts, the
prophet Micah declared that there is no other God
like Jehovah, the God of the Bible, *"because he delighteth in lovingkindness"* (Mic. 7:18 ASV), and He
shows it by the fact that He *"pardoneth iniquity,
and passeth over the transgression of the remnant of
his heritage"* (v. 18 ASV), that is, Israel.

The book of Psalms is one continuous Hebrew
anthology of songs of praise to a God who is *"abundant in lovingkindness"* (Ps. 86:5 ASV). Moses, the
supposedly stern old lawgiver, and inspired prophets, sages, historians, and kings, join in the swelling
chorus.

Such is the God of the Bible, the God of the Old
Testament as well as the God of the New Testament,
a very different God from what many modern, popular preachers declare the God of the Old Testament to

be. If these men would study the Old Testament more closely and thoroughly, and talk less about it until they do, it would be better for their own reputations for intelligent and thorough scholarship and impartiality. Moreover, it would be far better for their bewildered, confused, misled, and grievously wronged hearers. It is a case of the "blind leading the blind" and together falling into the ditch (Matt. 15:14)—the slimy and pernicious ditch of blasphemous dishonoring of God and His Word.

To Whom the Lovingkindness or Mercy of God Is Manifested

The question of to whom the lovingkindness of God is manifested is one that the Bible answers very plainly and with great fullness.

To Whomever He Wills

First of all, God's mercy is manifested to whomever He wills. He is absolutely sovereign in the exercise of His mercy. Jehovah Himself declared to Moses, as recorded in Exodus 33:19, *"I will be gracious to whom I will be gracious, and will show mercy on whom I will show mercy"* (ASV). The apostle Paul, after quoting in Romans 9:15 the above statement that Jehovah said to Moses, declared in Romans 9:18, *"Therefore He has mercy on whom He wills, and whom He wills He hardens."*

We should insist on this great truth that God is absolutely sovereign in the exercise of His mercy, that His mercy is exercised toward whomever He wills, that no one can dictate to Him as to whom He will have mercy upon. However, we should at the same time remember that, in point of fact, He wills to have mercy upon all whom He can have mercy upon. Peter put it in this way in 2 Peter 3:9,

> *The Lord is not slack concerning His promise, as some count slackness, but is longsuffering toward us, not willing that any should perish but that all should come to repentance.*

To Those Who Fear or Love Him

In the second place, God's lovingkindness is manifested toward those who fear or love Him, toward His servants who walk before Him with all their hearts. We read, in one of the earliest books of the Bible, in Deuteronomy 7:9:

> *Know therefore that Jehovah thy God, he is God, the faithful God, who keepeth covenant and lovingkindness with them that love him and keep his commandments to a thousand generations.* (ASV)

And in the second book of the Bible, in Exodus 20:5–6, we read:

> *Thou shalt not bow down thyself unto them, nor serve them* [idols]; *for I Jehovah thy God am a jealous God, visiting the iniquity of the fathers upon the children, upon the third and upon the fourth generation of them that hate me, and showing lovingkindness unto thousands* ["a thousand generations," ASV, margin] *of them that love me and keep my*

commandments.   *(Exod. 20:5–6 ASV)*

In the very familiar Psalm 103, we read:

> *For as the heavens are high above the earth, so great is his lovingkindness toward them that fear him....But the lovingkindness of Jehovah is from everlasting to everlasting upon them that fear him, and his righteousness unto children's children; to such as keep his covenant, and to those that remember his precepts to do them.*   *(vv. 11, 17–18 ASV)*

In 2 Chronicles 6:14, we read:

> *And* [Solomon] *said, O Jehovah, the God of Israel, there is no God like thee, in heaven, or on earth; who keepest covenant and lovingkindness with thy servants, that walk before thee with all their heart.*   *(ASV)*

We should keep in mind that the phrases, *"the fear of the LORD* [Jehovah]," used in the Old Testament, and *"the love of God,"* used in the New Testament, are practically synonymous. This may be seen by a comparison of Proverbs 8:13 and Proverbs 16:6 with 1 John 5:3. In Proverbs 8:13, we read: *"The fear of the LORD is to hate evil,"* and in Proverbs 16:6, we read: *"In mercy and truth Atonement is provided for iniquity; and by the fear of the LORD one departs from evil."* Now, in 1 John 5:3, we read: *"For this is the love of God, that we keep His commandments."*

So we see that the two phrases, *"the fear of the LORD"* and *"the love of God,"* describe nearly the same thing, although viewed from different standpoints. The two phrases look at practically the same attitude of mind toward God from different points of view.

To Those Who Confess and Forsake Their Sins

In the third place, the mercy of God is manifested toward everyone who confesses and forsakes his sins. We are told this in Proverbs 28:13: *"He who covers his sins will not prosper, but whoever confesses and forsakes them will have mercy."*

God shows mercy toward the vilest sinner if he confesses and forsakes his sin; but if he seeks to hide or deny his sins, he will find no mercy. If we seek to cover up our sins from God, He will uncover them to the whole world and severely punish them. But if we uncover them to God and forsake them, God will cover them up to such a depth that no one can ever find them. He will cover them with the atoning blood of Jesus Christ, which will hide them even from His own all-seeing eye. (See Psalm 103:12; Isaiah 38:17; 43:25; Romans 3:23–26.)

To Those Who Trust in Him

In the fourth place, the lovingkindness of God is manifested toward the one who trusts in the Lord. We are told this in Psalm 32:10: *"Many sorrows shall be to the wicked; but he that trusteth in Jehovah, lovingkindness shall compass him about"* (ASV). If a person will only put his whole trust in Jehovah, the true God of the Bible, then he will not only find lovingkindness from God, but he will also find that the *"lovingkindness shall compass him about* [surround him]" on every hand, and the Enemy will not be able to get to him at any point.

To Those Who Call Upon Him

In the fifth place, the lovingkindness of God is manifested toward all who call upon Him. We are told this in Psalm 86:5: *"For thou, Lord, art good, and ready to forgive, and abundant in lovingkindness unto all them that call upon thee"* (ASV). We find the same thought, though expressed in other words (the words *mercy* or *lovingkindness* are not used, but the thought is still there) in the New Testament, in Romans 10:12–13:

> For there is no distinction between Jew and Greek, for the same Lord over all is rich to all who call upon Him. For "whoever calls on the name of the LORD shall be saved."

HOW THE LOVINGKINDNESS OF GOD IS MANIFESTED

We come now to the last question, and it is a very practical question, How is the lovingkindness of God manifested? The teaching of the Bible on this point is also very full and very rich.

God Pardons Sin When It Is Confessed and Forsaken

In the first place, the lovingkindness of God is manifested in His pardoning sin when it is confessed and forsaken. We are told this over and over again in the Bible. For example, we read in Exodus 34:6–7:

And Jehovah passed by before [Moses], and proclaimed, Jehovah, Jehovah, a God merciful and gracious, slow to anger, and abundant in lovingkindness and truth; keeping loving-kindness for thousands, forgiving iniquity and transgression and sin; and that will by no means clear the guilty, visiting the iniquity of the fathers upon the children, and upon the children's children, upon the third and upon the fourth generation.   (Exod. 34:6–7 ASV)

One of the most familiar and, at the same time, clearest and most forceful expressions of this precious truth is found in Isaiah 55:7:

Let the wicked forsake his way, and the un-righteous man his thoughts; let him return to the LORD, and He will have mercy on him; and to our God, for He will abundantly pardon.

To backsliding Israel, Jehovah said in Jeremiah 3:12–13,

Go and proclaim these words toward the north, and say: "Return, backsliding Israel," says the LORD; "I will not cause My anger to fall on you. For I am merciful," says the LORD; "I will not remain angry forever. Only ac-knowledge your iniquity, that you have trans-gressed against the LORD your God."

In Jonah 4:2, we read:

So [Jonah] prayed to the LORD, and said, "...I know that You are a gracious and merciful

*God, slow to anger and abundant in loving-
kindness, One who relents from doing harm."*
(Jonah 4:2)

The prophet Micah proclaimed the truth that
the lovingkindness of Jehovah manifests itself in
pardoning iniquity, in one of the most beautiful passages in his prophecy, a prophecy that abounds in
marvelously beautiful passages:

*Who is a God like unto thee, that pardoneth
iniquity, and passeth over the transgression of
the remnant of his heritage? he retaineth not
his anger for ever, because he delighteth in lovingkindness.*   *(Mic. 7:18 ASV)*

David, who had fallen into his gross and appalling
sins of adultery and murder, still counted on the forgiveness of Jehovah because he had learned Jehovah's lovingkindness and mercy. Therefore, we read
this prayer in his Penitential Psalm as he makes full
confession of his sin: *"Have mercy upon me, O God,
according to Your lovingkindness; according to the
multitude of Your tender mercies, blot out my trans-
gressions"* (Ps. 51:1).

And Moses, as far back as thirty-four hundred
years ago, counting on the lovingkindness of Jehovah, pleaded with Him to forgive the frequently re-
peated sin and unfaithfulness of His people, as we
read in Numbers 14:17–20:

[Moses said to the Lord,] *Thou hast spoken,
saying, Jehovah is slow to anger, and abundant
in lovingkindness, forgiving iniquity and*

*transgression; and that will by no means clear
the guilty, visiting the iniquity of the fathers
upon the children, upon the third and upon the
fourth generation. Pardon, I pray thee, the iniquity of this people according unto the greatness of thy lovingkindness, and according as
thou hast forgiven this people, from Egypt even
until now. And Jehovah said, I have pardoned
according to thy word.   (Num. 14:17–20 ASV)*

Mercy has been defined by a great thinker and
theologian, Charles G. Finney, in these words: "Mercy
is exercised only where there is guilt." Now, this is
true in law, and in the usage of the word *mercy* in
law, but it is not true of the biblical usage of the
words *"mercy"* and *"lovingkindness,"* as is clear
from many of the passages to which I have already
referred. Nevertheless, it is true that mercy, or lovingkindness, is manifested in the forgiveness of sins.
This manifestation of mercy lies at the foundation of
many other manifestations of God's mercy in His
dealings with men. For the human race is a guilty
race, and when men recognize their guilt and confess
their sins, then they are most likely to see God's
lovingkindness manifested in a multitude of gracious
ways.

God Bears Long with Sinners

In the second place, the lovingkindness of God is
manifested in His bearing long with sinners, even
when they become stiff-necked and persist in sin. We
have a striking illustration of God's patience in His
dealings with constantly backsliding and rebellious

Israel. Read, for example, these verses from Nehemiah 9:

> [The Levites and others prayed,] *"But* [the Israelites in the time of Moses] *and our fathers acted proudly, hardened their necks, and did not heed Your commandments. They refused to obey, and they were not mindful of Your wonders that You did among them. But they hardened their necks, and in their rebellion they appointed a leader to return to their bondage. But You are God, ready to pardon, gracious and merciful, slow to anger, abundant in kindness, and did not forsake them.... Nevertheless they were disobedient and rebelled against You, cast Your law behind their backs and killed Your prophets, who testified against them to turn them to Yourself; and they worked great provocations. Therefore You delivered them into the hand of their enemies, who oppressed them; and in the time of their trouble, when they cried to You, You heard from heaven; and according to Your abundant mercies You gave them deliverers who saved them from the hand of their enemies....Yet for many years You had patience with them, and testified against them by Your Spirit in Your prophets. Yet they would not listen; therefore You gave them into the hand of the peoples of the lands. Nevertheless in Your great mercy You did not utterly consume them nor forsake them; for You are God, gracious and merciful."*
>
> (Neh. 9:16–17, 26–27, 30–31)

Over and over again, Israel departed from God, and He chastened them severely; but He did not forsake them. Israel has been frightfully chastened and scourged during the terrible centuries since they crucified their *"Lord and Christ"* (Acts 2:36), but *God has never forsaken them.* Their preservation and prosperity in the midst of the continued persecution and appalling calamities that have befallen them is the miracle of history.

As a nation, Israel is still untrue to Jehovah, the God of the Bible, and His Christ; and God is chastening them and scourging them to this day. What appalling things they are suffering today, and the worst is yet to come, *"the time of Jacob's trouble"* (Jer. 30:7). But again, Jehovah has not forsaken them and will bring them out in the end as the transcendently glorious nation of all nations. His lovingkindness makes that absolutely sure, and His Word makes it absolutely certain.

God Delivers from Sickness, Sorrow, and Oppression

In the third place, the lovingkindness of God is manifested in His delivering from sickness, sorrow, and oppression. We find this blessed truth in both the Old Testament and the New. For example, read the following passages:

> *O Jehovah, rebuke me not in thine anger, neither chasten me in thy hot displeasure. Have mercy upon me, O Jehovah; for I am withered away: O Jehovah, heal me; for my bones are troubled. My soul also is sore troubled: and thou, O Jehovah, how long? Return, O Jehovah, deliver my soul: save me for thy lovingkindness' sake.* (Ps. 6:1–4 ASV)

226

For indeed he [Paul's fellow worker Epaphroditus] *was sick almost unto death; but God had mercy on him, and not only on him but on me also, lest I should have sorrow upon sorrow.* *(Phil. 2:27)*

Thou in thy lovingkindness hast led the people that thou hast redeemed: thou hast guided them in thy strength to thy holy habitation. The peoples have heard, they tremble: pangs have taken hold on the inhabitants of Philistia. Then were the chiefs of Edom dismayed; the mighty men of Moab, trembling taketh hold upon them: all the inhabitants of Canaan are melted away. Terror and dread falleth upon them; by the greatness of thine arm they are as still as a stone; till thy people pass over, O Jehovah, till the people pass over that thou hast purchased. Thou wilt bring them in, and plant them in the mountain of thine inheritance, the place, O Jehovah, which thou hast made for thee to dwell in, the sanctuary, O Lord, which thy hands have established. Jehovah shall reign for ever and ever. *(Exod. 15:13–18 ASV)*

God Maintains the Security of Those Who Trust in Him

In the fourth place, the lovingkindness of God is manifested in His maintaining the security of those who trust in Him. David told us this in Psalm 21:7: *"For the king trusteth in Jehovah; and through the lovingkindness of the Most High he shall not be moved"* (ASV).

227

Not only the king, but the King of Kings, Jesus, will be so established that all the powers of Satan cannot move Him, because He *"trusteth in Jehovah."* However, even the least of God's own who trust in Him cannot be moved, because *"the lovingkindness of the Most High"* is on their side.

God Acts as a Defense and Refuge

In the fifth place, the lovingkindness of God is manifested in His acting as a defense and refuge in the day of trouble. David, the sweet singer of Israel, sang in Psalm 59:16,

> *But I will sing of thy strength; yea, I will sing aloud of thy lovingkindness in the morning: for thou hast been my high tower, and a refuge in the day of my distress.* (ASV)

If we, in spite of all our weaknesses and failures, put our trust in Jehovah and live for Him as David did, in spite of all his weaknesses, failures, and appalling lapses, then we, too, can be sure that the lovingkindness of Jehovah will manifest itself in His being our all-sufficient defense and our perfectly secure refuge and hiding place in every day of trouble and distress.

And now I reluctantly close our study of the lovingkindness of Jehovah, the God of the Bible. Who would give up such a God for the paltry gods of Christian Science or Theosophy or New Thought or Spiritualism or Unitarianism or New Theology or modern philosophy or Modernism in general?

Chapter 12

GOD IS FAITHFUL

If we are faithless, He remains faithful;
He cannot deny Himself.
—2 Timothy 2:13

I think that comparatively few Christians have dwelt much on the faithfulness of God, and therefore very few of us realize the wealth of meaning that there is in the teaching of the Bible on this exceedingly precious and joy-inspiring subject. In the course of our study, we will consider quite a number of Scripture texts. In these passages, God reveals the truth about Himself regarding the many ways in which He manifests His faithfulness toward those who know Him and put their trust in Him. The consideration of these passages, as the Holy Spirit Himself interprets them to us, will help us to still further appreciate the meaning and force of that wonderful saying of our Lord Jesus found in John 17:3: *"And this is eternal life, that they may know You, the only true God, and Jesus Christ whom You have sent."*

Our first text is Deuteronomy 7:9:

Know therefore that Jehovah thy God, he is God, the faithful God, who keepeth covenant and lovingkindness with them that love him and keep his commandments to a thousand generations. (Deut. 7:9 ASV)

Now let us turn to another passage in this same wonderful book of Deuteronomy, which the Devil so hates (I suppose in part because it was the only book from which our Lord Jesus quoted when He had His conflict with him in the wilderness and so completely routed him). The so-called higher critics of the prevailing theological school of thought also very persistently attempt to disparage and discredit this book, but all regenerate people who intelligently study it esteem it very highly. The verse is Deuteronomy 32:4:

The Rock, his work is perfect; for all his ways are justice: a God of faithfulness and without iniquity, just and right is he. (ASV)

The King James Version translates this passage differently. It reads:

He is the Rock, his work is perfect: for all his ways are judgment: a God of truth and without iniquity, just and right is he.

However, the Hebrew word that is translated *"truth"* in the King James Version is precisely the same word that is elsewhere translated *"faithfulness,"* and of course it should be translated in that way here also, just as it is in the American Standard Edition of the Revised Version.

God Is Faithful

Now let us turn to the prophet Isaiah:

Thus says the LORD, the Redeemer of Israel,
their Holy One, to Him whom man despises, to
Him whom the nation abhors, to the Servant of
rulers: "Kings shall see and arise, princes also
shall worship, because of the LORD who is
faithful, the Holy One of Israel; and He has
chosen You."   *(Isa. 49:7)*

We next go to the New Testament, to 1 Corinthians 1:9:

God is faithful, by whom you were called into
the fellowship of His Son, Jesus Christ our
Lord.

In this first epistle to the Corinthians, the apostle Paul especially dwelled on the faithfulness of God, perhaps to encourage the believers there since some of their own number had proven so unfaithful. Let us turn to another passage from this book:

No temptation has overtaken you except such
as is common to man; but God is faithful, who
will not allow you to be tempted beyond what
you are able, but with the temptation will also
make the way of escape, that you may be able
to bear it.   *(1 Cor. 10:13)*

We will now look at two passages from Paul's epistles to the Thessalonians:

Now may the God of peace Himself sanctify
you completely; and may your whole spirit,

soul, and body be preserved blameless at the
coming of our Lord Jesus Christ. He who calls
you is faithful, who also will do it.

(1 Thess. 5:23–24)

But the Lord is faithful, who will establish you
and guard you from the evil one. (2 Thess. 3:3)

Next, we will turn from the apostle Paul to the
apostle John:

If we confess our sins, He is faithful and just
to forgive us our sins and to cleanse us from
all unrighteousness. *(1 John 1:9)*

Now let us go back to the prophets, to the words
of Jeremiah in Lamentations 3:22–23:

It is of Jehovah's lovingkindnesses that we are
not consumed, because His compassions fail
not. They are new every morning; great is thy
faithfulness. *(ASV)*

Our three remaining texts are from the book of
Psalms, the book that is so completely given up to
extolling the glorious attributes of Jehovah, the God
of the Bible. The first verse is Psalm 33:4:

For the word of Jehovah is right; and all his
work is done in faithfulness. *(ASV)*

In this verse, the King James Version again uses
"truth" instead of *"faithfulness."* However, in this
case, also, the Hebrew word rendered *"truth"* is the

word that is elsewhere rendered *"faithfulness,"* and is from the root that means "to be faithful."

Now turn to Psalm 36:5:

Thy lovingkindness, O Jehovah, is in the heavens; thy faithfulness reacheth unto the skies.   (ASV)

The King James Version of this verse reads:

Thy mercy, O LORD, is in the heavens; and thy faithfulness reacheth unto the clouds.

However, the Hebrew word translated *"clouds"* in this passage is not the one ordinarily used for clouds; it is the word always used for "sky" or "skies" in every instance where these words are found in the Old Testament.

Now, for our last text, let us turn to the longest chapter in the Bible, the psalm that is given up to a description and exaltation of the glories of God and of His Word:

Forever, O LORD, Your word is settled in heaven. Your faithfulness endures to all generations; You established the earth, and it abides.   (Ps. 119:89–90)

THE MEANING OF "FAITHFUL"

In seven of these twelve texts, the definite statement is made that God is faithful, and each of the remaining five texts emphasizes the fact of His

infinite and eternal faithfulness. Lawgivers, prophets, apostles, kings, and poets, all inspired by the
same Spirit of God, the Spirit of Truth, join in one
mighty, exultant anthem of praise to the faithfulness
of God, which *"endures to all generations"* (Ps.
119:90). But what do the words *"faithful"* and
"faithfulness" mean as they are used in the Bible?
By carefully searching the Scriptures, we get a clear,
unmistakable, and incontrovertible answer to this
important question.

In the first place, looking at the derivation of the
Hebrew words that are translated in this way in the
Old Testament, we find that they were derived from a
Hebrew verb, *aman* (from which our word *amen*—
meaning "verily," "truly," "certainly"—is derived).
This verb means "to prop," "to stay," or "to support."
In its reflexive and intransitive use, the word means
"to stay oneself," or "to be supported." Therefore, the
adjective *"faithful"* means, when applied to a person,
such a person as one may safely lean upon with all his
weight, or stay himself upon.

The Greek word translated *"faithful"* in the
New Testament means "worthy of trust," one who
can be relied upon. But this same Greek word is used
in the Septuagint (the Greek translation of the Hebrew Bible that was in common use when the New
Testament was written) to translate the Hebrew
word already referred to, and of course gets its New
Testament meaning from that fact.

In the second place, looking at the usage of the
word *"faithful"* in both the Old Testament and the
New, we find that its biblical usage conforms exactly
to its derivation. For example, in Psalm 119:86, we
read, *"All Your commandments are faithful,"*

meaning that the commandments of God can be absolutely depended upon. In Proverbs 14:5, we read, *"A faithful witness does not lie, but a false witness will utter lies,"* meaning that a faithful witness is one who always tells the truth and who therefore can, under all circumstances, be depended upon.

Turning to the New Testament, to Jesus Christ's own use of the word, we read:

> *Who then is a faithful and wise servant, whom his master made ruler over his household, to give them food in due season? Blessed is that servant whom his master, when he comes, will find so doing.* (Matt. 24:45–46)

Here we see that a *faithful* servant is one who can be depended upon to do what he is told to do.

In Matthew 25:21, we read:

> *His lord said to him, "Well done, good and faithful servant; you were faithful over a few things, I will make you ruler over many things. Enter into the joy of your lord."*

We find almost exactly the same wording in verse twenty-three:

> *His lord said to him, "Well done, good and faithful servant; you have been faithful over a few things, I will make you ruler over many things. Enter into the joy of your lord."*

In these two verses, the word *"faithful"* is used four times. In each instance, it is used to describe a servant who can be absolutely depended upon, not only to do what he is told to do but also what ought to be done, whether he is told to do it or not.

Turning to the words of the apostle Paul, we read, in 1 Timothy 1:15: *"This is a faithful saying and worthy of all acceptance, that Christ Jesus came into the world to save sinners."* Here *"faithful"* is used to describe the character of this wonderful and apparently incredible statement that is made. The thought is that, as astonishing as the statement is, it is to be absolutely depended upon, it is *"worthy of all* [unhesitating and wholehearted] *acceptance."*

Now, looking to the last book in the Bible, we read: *"Then He who sat on the throne said, 'Behold, I make all things new.' And He said to me, 'Write, for these words are true and faithful'"* (Rev. 21:5). This verse tells us that the words that God has spoken are to be absolutely depended upon. It is clear, then, that the word *"faithful,"* as applied to a person, means a person upon whom we can support ourselves, a person who can be absolutely depended upon in any and every emergency that can arise. Therefore, to say "God is faithful" means that God is such a person—the kind of person whom we can absolutely rely upon in every emergency of life, the kind of person upon whom we can support ourselves under all circumstances, in time and in eternity. As Isaiah put it,

> *Thou wilt keep him in perfect peace, whose mind is stayed on thee; because he trusteth in thee. Trust ye in Jehovah for ever; for in Jehovah, even Jehovah, is an everlasting rock.*
> *(Isa. 26:3–4 ASV)*

God Is Faithful

The Bible has much to say that is indicative, instructive, and heart-thrilling about the measureless extent and eternal duration of the faithfulness of God. For example, read these passages again:

It is of Jehovah's lovingkindnesses that we are not consumed, because His compassions fail not. They are new every morning; great is thy faithfulness.   (Lam. 3:22–23 ASV)

Thy lovingkindness, O Jehovah, is in the heavens; thy faithfulness reacheth unto the skies.   (Ps. 36:5 ASV)

For the word of Jehovah is right; and all his work is done in faithfulness.   (Ps. 33:4 ASV)

Forever, O LORD, Your word is settled in heaven. Your faithfulness endures to all generations; You established the earth, and it abides.   (Ps. 119:89–90)

HOW THE FAITHFULNESS OF GOD IS MANIFESTED

Now, for our encouragement, for our deliverance from all fear, anxiety, and worry, and for our exceeding great joy, let us look at the many ways in which the faithfulness of God is manifested, as they are set forth in God's own Word about Himself, the Bible.

God Keeps His Word

In the first place, God's faithfulness is manifested in His keeping His promises and covenant to the very letter, in His fulfilling every word that goes out of His mouth, regardless of what man does. We see this truth in Hebrews 10:23, 36–37:

> *Let us hold fast the confession of our hope without wavering, for He who promised is faithful....For you have need of endurance, so that after you have done the will of God, you may receive the promise: "For yet a little while, and He who is coming will come and will not tarry."*

Here we are told that we do not need to have any fear whatsoever about the future, no matter how uncertain and threatening it may seem, because God's promises cover it all. *"He who promised is faithful,"* and therefore we may rest absolutely confident that His promises will be fulfilled to the very letter.

In a similar way, Moses comforted Israel in anticipation of all that their mighty enemies would do to overthrow and destroy them. He said in Deuteronomy 7:9,

> *Know therefore that Jehovah thy God, he is God, the faithful God, who keepeth covenant and lovingkindness with them that love him and keep his commandments to a thousand generations.* (ASV)

In much the same way, Solomon, in his prayer at the dedication of the temple at Jerusalem, in speaking to Jehovah, the God of Israel, exclaimed,

> *LORD God of Israel, there is no God in heaven above or on earth below like You, who keep Your covenant and mercy with Your servants who walk before You with all their hearts. You have kept what You promised Your servant David my father; You have both spoken with Your mouth and fulfilled it with Your hand, as it is this day.* (1 Kings 8:23–24)

Solomon reaffirmed the faithfulness of God as he closed this prayer. After referring to the calamities that would surely come upon Israel because of forsaking Jehovah, and of the way of deliverance by turning to and appealing to Jehovah, the only true God, he exclaimed,

> *Blessed be the LORD, who has given rest to His people Israel, according to all that He promised. There has not failed one word of all His good promise, which He promised through His servant Moses.* (v. 56)

Jehovah God Himself, after telling the Israelites of the terrible calamities that would surely come upon them if they forsook Him—

> *If [David's] sons forsake My law and do not walk in My judgments, if they break My statutes and do not keep My commandments, then I will punish their transgression with the rod, and their iniquity with stripes.* (Ps. 89:30–32)

—then declared,

Nevertheless My lovingkindness I will not utterly take from him, nor allow My faithfulness to fail. My covenant I will not break, nor alter the word that has gone out of My lips.

(Ps. 89:33–34)

God Delivers in Times of Greatest Trial

In the second place, God's faithfulness is manifested in the defense and deliverance of His servants in times of fiercest trial, testing, and conflict. We are told this by Peter in 1 Peter 4:19: *"Therefore let those who suffer according to the will of God commit their souls to Him in doing good, as to a faithful Creator."*

Etham, the Ezrahite, sang in Psalm 89:20–26,

[God said,] *"I have found My servant David; with My holy oil I have anointed him, with whom My hand shall be established; also My arm shall strengthen him. The enemy shall not outwit him, nor the son of wickedness afflict him. I will beat down his foes before his face, and plague those who hate him. But My faithfulness and My mercy shall be with him, and in My name his horn shall be exalted. Also I will set his hand over the sea, and his right hand over the rivers. He shall cry to Me, 'You are my Father, my God, and the rock of my salvation.'"*

This whole Eighty-ninth Psalm, which has fifty-two stanzas in all, might well be called the Faithfulness Psalm. It begins with these words, *"I will sing of the*

mercies ["lovingkindness,"* ASV] of the LORD forever;
with my mouth will I make known Your faithfulness
to all generations"* (v. 1), and it closes with the words
"Amen and Amen" (v. 52). Remember that *amen* is
derived from the verb from which the adjective
"faithful" and the noun *"faithfulness"* are derived.
The adverb is *amen* and the verb is *aman*.

God Is Faithful, Even When We Are Unfaithful

Third, God's faithfulness is manifested in His
standing by His people and saving them, even when
they are unfaithful to Him. We are told this fact in
both the Old Testament and the New. For example,
there is Jeremiah's song of heartbreaking sympathy
for Israel in the dire calamities that overtook them in
his day. He had foretold these calamities but did not
glory in the fact that his predictions had been fulfilled; indeed, he was heartbroken over the fact. Yet
we read these words in the midst of this most pathetic
dirge that was ever written:

> *It is of Jehovah's lovingkindnesses that we are
> not consumed, because His compassions fail
> not. They are new every morning; great is thy
> faithfulness.*   *(Lam. 3:22–23 ASV)*

In the book bearing his name, Jeremiah also cried
out, *"For Israel is not forsaken, nor Judah, by his
God, the LORD of hosts, though their land was filled
with sin against the Holy One of Israel"* (Jer. 51:5).
Israel had indeed been faithless, but God had continued to be faithful. And Israel as a nation is faithless to

this very day, but God still continues to be faithful and will even yet make Israel glorious.

The prophet Samuel proclaimed the same truth in his day when the people and their priests and prophets had been grossly wicked and faithless to God. We see this in 1 Samuel 12:20–22:

> Then Samuel said to the people, "Do not fear. You have done all this wickedness; yet do not turn aside from following the LORD, but serve the LORD with all your heart. And do not turn aside; for then you would go after empty things which cannot profit or deliver, for they are nothing. For the LORD will not forsake His people, for His great name's sake, because it has pleased the LORD to make you His people."

And the apostle Paul declared the same truth to us who are believers in Jesus Christ and who still are often a faithless company. He said in 2 Timothy 2:13, "If we are faithless, He remains faithful; He cannot deny Himself." Oh, I do rejoice that my security, here and hereafter, is not dependent upon my faithfulness, but upon His.

God Provides a Way of Escape from Temptation

Fourth, God's faithfulness is manifested in His not allowing His children to be tempted above what they are able to stand. We read this blessed promise in these very familiar words of 1 Corinthians 10:13:

> No temptation has overtaken you except such as is common to man; but God is faithful, who

> *will not allow you to be tempted beyond what*
> *you are able, but with the temptation will also*
> *make the way of escape, that you may be able*
> *to bear it.*   *(1 Cor. 10:13)*

What strength these words have been to a multitude of Christians who deeply felt their own weaknesses but supported themselves on God's faithfulness. His faithfulness is manifested in His making a way of escape so that we may be able to bear temptation.

God Establishes Us in Him Forever

Fifth, the faithfulness of God is manifested in His confirming and establishing those whom He has called; guarding them from the Evil One so that not one of them will ever perish; and sanctifying them wholly and preserving them entirely—spirit, soul, and body—without blame at the coming of the Lord Jesus Christ. We find this precious truth presented very clearly in three different passages from Paul's epistles. The first is 1 Corinthians 1:8–9:

> [The Lord Jesus Christ] *will also confirm you*
> *to the end, that you may be blameless in the*
> *day of our Lord Jesus Christ. God is faithful,*
> *by whom you were called into the fellowship of*
> *His Son, Jesus Christ our Lord.*

The second is 2 Thessalonians 3:3:

> *The Lord is faithful, who will establish you*
> *and guard you from the evil one.*

Third, and best of all, is 1 Thessalonians 5:23–24:

> *Now may the God of peace Himself sanctify you completely; and may your whole spirit, soul, and body be preserved blameless at the coming of our Lord Jesus Christ. He who calls you is faithful, who also will do it.*

The faithfulness of God makes it certain that, at the return of our Lord Jesus to this earth, we will be sanctified wholly, and that our *"whole spirit, soul, and body* [will] *be preserved blameless."* Therefore, is it any wonder that, on the one hand, we *"rejoice with joy inexpressible and full of glory"* (1 Pet. 1:8) in His faithfulness, and, on the other hand, eagerly cry out, *"Amen. Even so, come, Lord Jesus!"* (Rev. 22:20)? This last prayer in the Bible begins with the word *"Amen."* Remember that the Hebrew root of *"Amen"* is the same root from which the Hebrew words translated *"faithful"* and *"faithfulness"* are derived.

Our Lord Jesus Himself said in John 10:28–29,

> *And I give them eternal life, and they shall never perish; neither shall anyone snatch them out of My hand. My Father, who has given them to Me, is greater than all; and no one is able to snatch them out of My Father's hand.*

As believers in Jesus Christ, all our confidence in regard to the future, both for this present age and for the age that is to come, is not in our faithfulness but in His. Dr. A. T. Pierson was once asked if he believed in the perseverance of the saints. He replied, "No, I don't; but I do believe in the perseverance of the Savior."

God Chastens Us When We Go Astray

Sixth, God's faithfulness is manifested in His chastening His children when they go astray. We read this in Psalm 119:75: *"I know, O LORD, that Your judgments are right, and that in faithfulness You have afflicted me."* If God only showered blessings upon us and never let suffering, yes, keen suffering and anguish come into our lives, He would not be a *faithful* God, a God to be absolutely depended upon in every contingency. For we often need sorrow far more than we need joy, and our faithful God sends it. As we read in Hebrews 12:6, *"For whom the LORD loves He chastens, and scourges every son whom He receives."*

God Forgives Our Sins When We Confess Them

Seventh, God's faithfulness is manifested in His forgiving His children when they confess their sins. John told us this in 1 John 1:9: *"If we confess our sins, He is faithful and just to forgive us our sins and to cleanse us from all unrighteousness."* Our confidence that God will forgive our sins when we confess them rests upon two known facts about God; namely, God is righteous and God is faithful. God's righteousness pledges Him to forgive our sins because He Himself has provided an atonement for them that perfectly satisfies the demands of His own righteousness and holiness. God is righteous, and therefore He will not require payment twice. Moreover, God's faithfulness makes it absolutely certain that He will forgive believers' sins when they are confessed; for He has promised to do it, and His faithfulness makes it absolutely certain that He will keep His Word. If you are a believer in Jesus Christ, for you to doubt that your sin is forgiven when you have confessed it is to question both the righteousness and faithfulness of God, as well as to question His veracity. Therefore, to question that your sins are forgiven is not proper humility but daring presumption.

God Answers the Prayers of His Children

Eighth, God's faithfulness is manifested in His answering the prayers of His children. We are taught this in Psalm 143:1–2:

> *Hear my prayer, O LORD, give ear to my supplications! In Your faithfulness answer me, and in Your righteousness. Do not enter into judgment with Your servant, for in Your sight no one living is righteous.*

THERE IS NO OTHER GOD LIKE THE GOD OF THE BIBLE

The last three chapters of this book have been on the righteousness, the lovingkindness (or mercy), and the faithfulness of God. These three attributes of God run along very nearly parallel lines, and they are all pledged to the deliverance, the defense, and the complete and eternal salvation of God's people.

Such is the God of the Bible. What a wonderful God! We can well exclaim with Micah of old, *"Who is*

a God like You?" (Mic. 7:18). And the answer is: No
other god is like the God of the Bible, the God of the
Old Testament and the New Testament, the God of
Abraham, Isaac, and Jacob, who is the same God as
the God of Paul, Peter, John, James, and of our Lord
and Savior Jesus Christ.

One thing must have impressed you as we have
studied the God of the Bible in these twelve chapters: the marvelous unity of the Bible, with its forty
or more human authors, all of them God-controlled,
presenting, through more than fifteen hundred
years and under the most diverse and divergent circumstances, the same God in every respect. This fact
conclusively proves that it was one Supreme Mind—
and no less a mind than the mind of the one Infinite,
Eternal, and Omniscient God—who spoke through
them all.

Yes, *"who is a God like* [Him]?" (Mic. 7:18).
Surely not the god of ancient philosophers, poets,
and sages; and just as surely not the god of modern
philosophers, poets, and dreamers, except insofar
as they have borrowed their ideas of God from this
centuries-old Book—some parts thirty-four centuries old and yet always presenting the same God.
The god of Christian Science is not like Him. The
god of Theosophy is not like Him. The god of New
Thought is not like Him. The god of Spiritualism is
not like Him. The god of modern Unitarianism is
not like Him. The god of New Theology is not like
Him. The god of modern philosophy is not like
Him. The god of Modernism, in all its forms, is not
like Him. Therefore, let us cast away these
man-made gods. Let us believe in, obey, surrender

our lives to, and worship and adore the God of the Bible. And let us continue to study to know Him ever more and more fully, for *"this is eternal life, that they may know You, the only true God, and Jesus Christ whom You have sent"* (John 17:3).

About the Author

Reuben Archer Torrey was born in Hoboken, New Jersey, on January 28, 1856. He graduated from Yale University in 1875 and from Yale Divinity School in 1878.

Upon his graduation, R. A. Torrey became a Congregational minister. A few years later, he joined Dwight L. Moody in his evangelistic work in Chicago and became the pastor of the Chicago Avenue Church. He was selected by D. L. Moody to become the first dean of the Moody Bible Institute of Chicago. Under his direction, Moody Institute became a pattern for Bible institutes around the world.

Torrey is respected as one of the greatest evangelists of modern times. At the turn of the century, Torrey began his evangelistic tours and crusades. He spent the years of 1903–1905 in a worldwide revival campaign, along with the famous song leader Charles McCallon Alexander. Together they ministered in many parts of the world and reportedly brought nearly one hundred thousand souls to Jesus. Torrey continued worldwide crusades for the next fifteen years, eventually reaching Japan and China. During those same years, he served as Dean of the Bible Institute of Los Angeles and pastored the Church of the Open Door in that city.

Torrey longed for more Christian workers to take an active part in bringing the message of salvation through Christ to a lost and dying world. His straightforward style of evangelism has shown thousands of Christian workers how to become effective soulwinners.

R. A. Torrey died on October 26, 1928. He is well-remembered today for his inspiring devotional books on the Christian life, which have been translated into many different languages. In *The God of the Bible,* Torrey's complete devotion to the one true God is clearly evident. It was this love for God and for His Son, our Savior Jesus Christ, that sent Torrey around the world to bring men, women, and children to salvation in Christ. His books continue to minister to believers today, inspiring them to love and serve God with wholehearted dedication.